THE EUCHARIST
IS REALLY JESUS

THE
EUCHARIST
IS REALLY
JESUS

How Christ's Body and Blood
Are the Key to Everything We Believe

JOE HESCHMEYER

Catholic
Answers
Press

Published by

Catholic Answers, Inc.
2020 Gillespie Way
El Cajon, California 92020

1-888-291-8000 orders
619-387-0042 fax
catholic.com

978-1-68357-307-4
978-1-68357-308-1 Kindle
978-1-68357-309-8 ePub

To my wife Anna,
for nourishing our children with your body and blood.

Contents

Introduction

The Breaking of the Bread
and the Lamb Standing as Though Slain

On Easter morning, two disciples of Jesus are on their way from Jerusalem back to Emmaus. They might be husband and wife, but the text doesn't say for certain. St. Luke only names one of the two: Cleopas. If they *are* a married couple, they might be Jesus' aunt and uncle. (Hegesippus, a Christian writer from the second century, references "the Lord's uncle, Clopas."[1]) If Cleopas and Clopas are the same person, then we know his wife is Mary, one of the women who was at the Crucifixion (John 19:25), and that they have children named James and Joses (Mark 15:40), who are referred to as "brothers" of Jesus (Mark 6:3).*

Whatever the case, these two disciples are walking the seven miles home from Jerusalem to Emmaus, "talking and discussing together," when another traveler joins them (Luke 24:15). Noticing their sadness, he asks what they're discussing, and they reply:

---

* Since Hebrew lacked a word for *cousins*, cousins could be referred to as "brothers," just as Abraham and Lot are called "brothers" in Genesis 13:8 and 14:14-16, despite being uncle and nephew.

Concerning Jesus of Nazareth, who was a prophet mighty in deed and word before God and all the people, and how our chief priests and rulers delivered him up to be condemned to death, and crucified him. But we had hoped that he was the one to redeem Israel. Yes, and besides all this, it is now the third day since this happened. Moreover, some women of our company amazed us. They were at the tomb early in the morning and did not find his body; and they came back saying that they had even seen a vision of angels, who said that he was alive. Some of those who were with us went to the tomb, and found it just as the women had said; but him they did not see (19-24).

If Cleopas and Clopas *are* the same person, his wife and likely walking companion was one of those "women of our company" who were the first witnesses of the empty tomb (Luke 24:10). The other traveler then replies, "O foolish men, and slow of heart to believe all that the prophets have spoken! Was it not necessary that the Christ should suffer these things and enter into his glory?" (25-26).

On arriving back in Emmaus, they invite the traveler to join them. There, while "at table with them, he took the bread and blessed, and broke it, and gave it to them. And their eyes were opened and they recognized him; and he vanished out of their sight" (30-31).

It's only here that Cleopas and his companion realize two things. First, that the traveler who had joined was Jesus (Luke explains that "their eyes were kept from recognizing him" in verse 16). Second, that Jesus had opened up the Old Testament scriptures to them in a radically new way: "Did not our hearts burn within us while he talked to us on the road, while he opened to us the scriptures?" (v. 32). They immediately arise and make the seven-mile journey back to Jerusalem, where they tell the apostles about how Jesus "was known to them in the breaking of the bread" (v. 35).

This is an important detail that we often overlook. Jesus is the key to unlocking the Old Testament scriptures: "beginning with Moses and all the prophets, he interpreted to them in all the scriptures the things concerning himself" (Luke 24:27). But they only realize who he is, and how he makes sense of Scripture, once they recognize him "in the breaking of the bread."

This expression is *eucharistic*: the "breaking of the bread" is how Luke describes the early Christian Eucharist (Acts 2:42, 46), and the way he describes this scene closely resembles the way he describes the Last Supper. Look at the careful way Luke presents this moment: Jesus "took the bread," "blessed" it, "broke it," and "gave it to them" (v. 30).

Why does Luke use four verbs to describe this moment? After all, presumably he knows we know how to eat bread, and he's not trying to reassure us that they said their prayers before eating.

It's not a coincidence that this is just how Luke and the other Evangelists recount Jesus' actions at the Last Supper. In Luke: "He took bread, and when he had given thanks he broke it and gave it to them, saying, 'This is my body which is given for you. Do this in remembrance of me'" (22:19). In Matthew: "Jesus took bread, and blessed, and broke it, and gave it to the disciples and said, 'Take, eat; this is my body'" (26:26). It's those same four actions again: Jesus *takes*, *blesses*, *breaks*, and *gives*. Jesus reveals himself and the scriptures are unlocked.

THE LAMB STANDING AS THOUGH SLAIN

We see this in another, more mystical way in the book of Revelation. St. John sees a scroll "sealed with seven seals" in "the right hand of him who was seated on the throne" (5:1). A "strong angel" proclaims with a loud voice, "Who is worthy to open the scroll and break its seals?" (v. 2). When "no one in heaven or on earth or under the earth" (v. 3) was able to open the scroll, John bursts into tears. One of the heavenly elders then says to him, "Weep not; lo, the Lion of the tribe of Judah, the Root of David, has conquered, so that he can open the scroll and its seven seals" (v. 5).

But what John sees next isn't a lion; it's a *lamb*. More specifically, "I saw a Lamb standing, as though it had been slain" (v. 6), who then takes the scroll, while heaven breaks out into a chorus: "Worthy art thou to take the scroll and to open its seals, for thou wast slain and by thy blood didst ransom men for God from every tribe and tongue and people and nation, and hast made them a kingdom and priests to our God, and they shall reign on earth" (vv. 9-10).

There's a tremendous irony in this passage. We expect the "strong angel" to be able to open the seals, but he can't: no creature can. And then we expect the Son of God to be able to open it because he's the conquering Lion of Judah. But Christ appears not in strength, but in humility: "a Lamb standing, as though it had been slain." Even this image is paradoxical: the slain are not known for standing upright. It's an image of Jesus conquering through his meekness and self-sacrifice and death.

But it's not only an image of Christ the crucified, but of Christ as the slain lamb, recalling both the Old Testament Passover and the Lord's Supper in which "Christ, our paschal lamb, has been sacrificed" (1 Cor. 5:7). So, it's only when we know Jesus Christ in *this* way that everything else is unlocked. Otherwise, some scrolls remain sealed off to our understanding. We don't get to experience our hearts burning within us.

The eucharistic Jesus is the key. That's the whole theme of this book. The Catholic understanding of the Eucharist is that Jesus *gives us himself* in the Eucharist. When we receive it, we receive him in his entirety. The Eucharist isn't *just* a symbol, or just Jesus' "spiritual presence." The Eucharist is really Jesus.

SEEING WITH NEW EYES

Sometimes, to increase our understanding, we don't need new *information* but a new way of *thinking* about the information that we already have. For instance, when Nicolaus Copernicus (1473–1543) first argued that the earth revolved around the sun, it wasn't because he was the first to discover the mathematical and astronomical problems with the idea of geocentrism (the idea that the sun revolves around the earth). Those problems had been recognized for a long time, but the mathematicians and astronomers before Copernicus had come up with clever ways of explaining the problems away. But Copernicus created a paradigm shift by offering a new way of addressing the problems that made better sense of the data.[2]

The same thing is true when we think about the Eucharist. We're not going to discover Bible verses that no one has ever heard before. But a proper interpretation of the Eucharist will make the best sense of the biblical data we have— *and* neatly connect aspects of the Faith that might otherwise seem disconnected. As C.S. Lewis once said, "I believe in Christianity as I believe that the Sun has risen, not only because I see it but because by it, I see everything else."[3] Likewise, the right understanding of the Eucharist is critical for "seeing" everything else in Christianity.

But before we get to that "everything else," let's start with a simple question: what's the right understanding of the Eucharist?

THE EUCHARIST
IS REALLY JESUS

1

What Catholics Believe About the Eucharist (and Why)

My old pastor gave a homily in which he talked about preparing a girl for First Communion. Her parents had been wondering if she was ready yet, so Father asked her to explain her understanding of the Eucharist. She pointed to the large crucifix in the back of church and said, "That looks like Jesus, but isn't. The Eucharist doesn't look like Jesus, but is." It's hard to imagine a better or more succinct way of capturing what Catholics believe about the Eucharist. Needless to say, the priest decided she was ready!

I have one other story, one of my experiences teaching in an "Inquiry" night at my parish in Kansas City. (Inquiry nights are for those who have questions about Catholicism but aren't necessarily ready to prepare to enter the Church.) One of the young women attending was coming from a

Lutheran background, and so she believed that Christ was "in, with, and under" the eucharistic bread, but the bread still remains bread. She wanted to know how this view, which is sometimes termed *consubstantiation*,[4] differed from the Catholic view, which is typically called *transubstantiation*.

Instead of getting into the technical discussion on "modes of presence," I asked her, "Do you worship the Eucharist?" She looked surprised and said she didn't."[5] And so I told her, "We do."

There's the difference. Catholics worship the Eucharist, and for a simple reason: we believe that the Eucharist is really Jesus. Not simply a symbol of Jesus, or Jesus' mysterious presence somehow lingering there with bread and wine, but *Jesus*.

I like how St. Cyril of Jerusalem explained it back in the fourth century. Preaching to a group of newly baptized Christians in the year 350, he tells them to be "fully assured that the seeming bread is not bread, though sensible to taste, but the body of Christ; and that the seeming wine is not wine, though the taste will have it so, but the blood of Christ."[6] After all, Cyril says, since Jesus Christ "declared and said of the bread, 'This is my body,' who shall dare to doubt any longer? And since he has himself affirmed and said, 'This is my blood,' who shall ever hesitate, saying, that it is not his blood?"[7]

That's it in a nutshell: the Eucharist doesn't look like Jesus, but it is.

A HARD SAYING

This is admittedly a strange teaching. Even many people today who pride themselves on being biblical "literalists" balk at taking Jesus' words about the Eucharist literally.* That's actually a good sign. The first people to hear Jesus spell out his eucharistic teaching responded by saying, "This is a hard saying; who can listen to it?" (John 6:60). So if your beliefs about the Eucharist *don't* cause this reaction, you probably don't believe the same thing Jesus taught.

This "hard saying" has generated a number of good questions. *Does this mean that whenever I receive the Eucharist, I'm chewing up part of Jesus' body?*[8] *Or that Jesus leaves heaven at every Mass?*[9] *Or that Jesus is united to bread and wine in the same way that his soul and body are united, or his humanity and divinity?*

These three not-unreasonable objections all make the same mistake: assuming that Jesus must be present in the Eucharist in the same way that he was present at, say, the Wedding of Cana. But we know that this is wrong.

There are different ways of being "present." If you're invited to a work meeting, you might attend in person. But if you're halfway around the country, you might instead attend by video conference. You're still "present" in a way, but not in the same way as the people there in person. You can see and hear everything, but you can't smell or touch anything. Or perhaps you're driving, and so you attend by phone. Now you can hear and speak, but you can't see. In neither of these cases are you simply absent from the meeting. You're present in some way: it's just that your "mode of presence" is different in each.

The Bible mentions several different ways that Jesus can

---

* For instance, on the same page that Roy Zuck argues that we should "always take a passage in its literal sense unless there is good reason for doing otherwise," he also claims that Jesus "obviously was speaking figuratively" in John 6:53-58. Roy Zuck, *Basic Bible Interpretation* (Wheaton: Victor Books, 1991), p. 146.

be "present." For instance, he's present in the "least of these" (Matt. 25:40), but not in the same way as when two or three are gathered in his name (Matt. 18:20). In yet another way, he is present in all things, and "in him all things hold to-gether" (Col. 1:16-17). He was holding all creation together in himself even as he walked the shores of Galilee. The same Jesus "lay in the manger without leaving heaven."[10]

In one way, at his ascension Christ left us to take his rightful place at the right hand of the Father. As the angel said, "This Jesus, who was taken up from you into heaven, will come in the same way as you saw him go into heaven" (Acts 1:11). And yet in other ways, he's still with us, which is why one of his final promises was "I am with you always, to the close of the age" (Matt. 28:20). One of the ways that he fulfills that promise is in his presence in the sacraments, particularly in the Eucharist.

So we might say that Jesus came in *history*, is still here in *mystery*, and is coming again in *majesty*.[11] Christ is bodily present in the Eucharist, but not in the same way that he will be when he comes again in glory.*

You might be wondering why, if Jesus is bodily present in the Eucharist, doesn't it look like him? In the Mass, bread and wine are brought forward to the altar. The priest prays over them, calling down the Holy Spirit, and then (follow-ing Jesus' instructions in Luke 22:19) the priest prays over the gifts in the person of Jesus, saying "this is my body" and "this is my blood." But nothing *appears* to happen. The Eu-charist looks, tastes, feels, and smells like simple bread and wine. And that's true: all of those things remain the same.

---

* Theologians distinguish this by contrasting what they call Jesus' *sacramen-tal* presence with his *local* presence.

So what changes? The Catholic belief about the Eucharist is sometimes called "transubstantiation" because we believe that the *substance* of bread and wine has changed into the body and blood of Christ, while the *accidents* of appearance, taste, etc.—things that are not necessary for the substance—remain.

Yes, these are philosophical terms that aren't in the Bible. But then, the idea that transubstantiation must be proven from the Bible alone, using all these exact words, misunderstands both the Bible and theology. The task of both theologians and preachers is to explain what the Bible means. And that requires, almost by definition, finding other words to help express or encapsulate biblical teachings. Otherwise, you're simply quoting, not explaining. And this is just as true when we're talking about the doctrine of the Trinity, the mysterious union of Christ's humanity and divinity, or the theology of the cross. Language and philosophy are tools we use to understand and explain biblical truth.

So what do philosophers mean by *substance* and *accidents*, then? Roughly speaking, substance is *what* something is, and accidents are *how* it is.

Your height and weight and everything else on your driver's license might help to *describe* you, but they don't *define* you. Who and what you are aren't reducible to the accidents of *how* you are. Accidents can, and often do, change: you change clothes, dye your hair, wear colored contacts, lose weight, get taller, grow older . . . and yet you're still you. Those are "accidental changes": your accidents have changed, but your substance is still you.

But other types of change are bigger than this, because things are created or destroyed. When a man and a woman procreate, their gametes (sperm and egg) produce something new: a human being that didn't exist before. That's a "substantial change": a new substance is here that wasn't here a moment ago.

In describing what happens in the Eucharist as "transubstantiation," we're saying two things. First, there's been a substantial change. Something—or rather, someone—is here who wasn't here a moment ago.* But, second, there isn't an accidental change. The accidents of bread and wine are the same before and after.[12]

As with mysteries like the Trinity, no analogy perfectly captures this divine reality. But if you'll forgive the potential silliness of the example, I find the old book (and subsequent movies) *Freaky Friday* helpful. The book opens with the 13-year-old protagonist Annabel Andrews explaining:

> *When I woke up this morning, I found I'd turned into my mother.* There I was, in my mother's bed, with my feet reaching all the way to the bottom; I had on my mother's nightgown and a ring on my left hand, I mean her left hand, and lumps and pins all over my head.[13]

From an outside perspective, what has changed? Not any of the accidents: the feet, nightgown, ring, hand, and hair rollers are all right where they were before. Externally, the appearances have remained the same. But there has been an enormous change in what we might call the inner reality: a person who wasn't there on Thursday is there on Friday. And that is (sort of) what happens at every Mass.

---

* Or, more specifically, wasn't here *in this way* a moment ago.

WHY CATHOLICS BELIEVE IN THE EUCHARIST

Why believe such a strange thing? It might help to answer that question in two halves. Why do we believe that the "appearances" of bread and wine remain? Because our senses tell us so. Why do we believe that there has been a miraculous change of substance? Because Jesus tells us so.

At the Last Supper, Jesus holds up what appears to be bread and wine, but then says, "Take, eat; this is my body," and then, "Drink of it, all of you; for this is my blood of the covenant, which is poured out for many for the forgiveness of sins" (Matt. 26:26-28). What does he mean by that? Does he mean that the bread and wine *signifies* or metaphorically represents his body, or does "is" really mean "is"?

Although we find plenty of instances in the Gospels where Jesus uses metaphorical language, it never sounds like what he says at the Last Supper. For example, he says, "I am the door of the sheep" (John 10:7). But he never goes over to a particular door, points to it, and says, "This is me now!" By itself, this difference doesn't prove that Jesus meant those words about his body and blood literally, but it should at least give us pause. If this *is* just a symbol, why doesn't he introduce it like any of his other symbols?

JESUS' SECOND-TO-LAST PASSOVER (JOHN 6)

We read of Jesus instituting the Eucharist in the Gospels of Matthew, Mark, and Luke, as well as in St. Paul's first letter to the Corinthians. John gives us something different, which is not surprising: John wrote his Gospel long after the other three, and he assumes you've read them already. His Gospel is meant as a sort of "gap-filler," covering important moments in the life of Jesus that nobody else had written down yet.[14] He offers us "the rest of the story."

Instead of focusing on the Eucharist at the Last Supper, John looks at Jesus' teaching a year earlier, in which he first broaches the idea of the Eucharist. In case we miss the connection, John tells us that "the Passover, the feast of the Jews, was at hand" (John 6:4), and we know that it's on the following Passover that Jesus will institute the Eucharist at the Last Supper.[15] I've mentioned this part of John's Gospel already—it's this teaching that Jesus' listeners declare a "hard saying"—but let's flesh it out a bit.

Before Jesus tells his listeners about the Eucharist, he introduces us to the idea in another way, by feeding 5,000 of them with five barley loaves. John tells us how Jesus "took the loaves, and when he had given thanks, he distributed them to those who were seated," with more than enough for all (v. 11). But those five English words "when he had given thanks" are a translation of just one Greek word: *eucharistēsas.* Jesus "eucharitizes" the bread, so to speak. He gives thanks over it.

Jesus isn't giving them the Eucharist here. It's still bread, but bread that's been miraculously multiplied through his prayerful thanksgiving, his *eucharistia,* so that it can do what would be otherwise physically impossible for five barley loaves.*

---

* The Protestant Reformer John Calvin argued that transubstantiation couldn't be true, claiming that it confuses Jesus' human and divine natures. Calvin is confused about Christ's mode of presence in the Eucharist. But in any event, you might just as well raise his same objection against the miraculously multiplied bread in John 6. In both cases, God is doing something miraculous, and otherwise impossible, in the material world.

After each of the multiplication miracles, Jesus has his followers gather up the leftovers (Matt. 14:20, 15:37; Mark 6:43, 8:8; Luke 9:17). That's not just good housekeeping: Jesus points out the symbolic significance of there being twelve baskets the first time and seven the second (Mark 8:19-21), since twelve and seven are important numbers in Judaism. John gives us the clearest indication of what's going on by reporting Jesus' instruction to the disciples: "Gather up the fragments left over, that nothing may be lost" (John 6:12). It seems that Jesus wants this transformed bread to be treated with reverence.

THE BREAD OF LIFE DISCOURSE

The next day, the crowds follow Jesus into Capernaum, no doubt hoping for more free food. (I think that anyone involved in ministry can attest to the draw of free food.) Jesus then begins what has become known as the *Bread of Life* discourse, in which he will describe his flesh and blood as real food and drink. As we delve more deeply into this, I want to acknowledge two things for the benefit of those who may be used to thinking of Jesus' words here simply as a metaphor for faith.

First, it's true that Jesus often *does* use metaphorical language, and his listeners (then as now) often err by taking him too literally. Earlier in the Gospel of John, Jesus says, "Destroy this temple, and in three days I will raise it up." The people take him to literally mean the temple in Jerusalem, and so John clarifies that "he spoke of the temple of his body" (John 2:19-21). Then, he tells Nicodemus that he has to be "born anew." Nicodemus takes him to refer to physical birth, but Jesus clarifies that he's talking about being "born of water and the Spirit" (John 3:3-5). After that, when he tells the Samaritan woman at the well about "living water," she takes him to literally mean water, but Jesus explains that "the water that I shall give" isn't like "this water" (John 4:10-15).

Second, it's true that part of what Jesus is doing here *is* using the imagery of eating as a way of speaking about faith. So why not just leave it at that, then: the Bread of Life discourse means nothing more than "believe in me, and you'll be saved"? Because it's clear from the text of John 6 that something more is going on.

The Bread of Life discourse is really a *dialogue* between Jesus and his listeners. He points out that they're after free food when they should be seeking "the food which endures to eternal life" (John 6:26-27). The people then demand a sign, and helpfully remind Jesus that Moses gave the Israelites bread from heaven to eat (vv. 30-31). Jesus tells them that "it was not Moses who gave you the bread from heaven; my Father gives you the true bread from heaven. For the bread of God is that which comes down from heaven, and gives life to the world," to which they reply, "Lord, give us this bread always" (vv. 32-34).

At this point, it's not entirely clear what the crowd is thinking: whether they're still looking for free food or whether they realize that Jesus is talking about something more than bread . . . something even greater than the heavenly manna that the Israelites ate in the desert.

In any case, Jesus clarifies that he's speaking about himself: "I am the bread of life; he who comes to me shall not hunger, and he who believes in me shall never thirst" (John 6:35). This is a clear shift in the conversation: now the crowd is not just trying to get free food, or free manna, or see a miracle. They're beginning to be unnerved by what Jesus is saying. John says that they "murmured at him," asking one another, "Is not this Jesus, the son of Joseph, whose father and mother we know? How does he now say, 'I have come down from heaven'?" (vv. 41–42).

In the first back-and-forth, they seemed to take the "bread" part literally, but didn't realize that Jesus was referring to himself. Now, they realize that Jesus *is* referring to himself, but they're now taking the "bread from heaven" part as a metaphor to mean simply that Jesus comes from heaven. At no point in the conversation so far have the people thought that Jesus was teaching them anything like the Eucharist. In fact, if those who take the Eucharist as a mere symbol are right, then Jesus' listeners have seemingly understood him correctly.

But Jesus makes it clear that there's more to his message that they're not getting. He then presents the hardest part of the Bread of Life discourse, where he says that all this talk about eating is more than metaphorical:

> I am the bread of life. Your fathers ate the manna in the wilderness, and they died. This is the bread which comes down from heaven, that a man may eat of it and not die. I am the living bread which came down from heaven; if any one eats of this bread, he will live for ever; and the bread which I shall give for the life of the world is my flesh (John 6:49–51).

Those last three words are shocking. If Jesus had said that the bread was *his teaching*, or was *faith*, or something else disembodied, it would be easy to square his message with the way many Protestants read John 6. But he doesn't say any of those things: he says that, yes, the bread *is* a metaphor . . . but a metaphor for *eating his flesh*.

It's only at this point that Jesus' listeners conclude that Jesus wants them literally to eat his body, and they're horrified, asking one another, "How can this man give us his flesh to eat?" (John 6:52).

It's striking that it has taken this long to get here. The Bread of Life discourse starts around John 6:26, and it's only now, in verse fifty-two, that they're asking this.

That's a noticeable contrast from John chapters 2, 3, and 4. In those cases, Jesus' audiences immediately misunderstood him by taking him too literally. In each of those cases, either Jesus or John just as immediately clarified that they weren't getting it. This time, the crowd took him *metaphorically* at first. They didn't initially think Jesus meant we were to eat his flesh . . . until Jesus slowly and deliberately led them to that interpretation.

And how does Jesus respond to their horror? Does he say, "No, no, you've misunderstood me once again"? Does he say, "You were right before, when you thought this was all a metaphor for believing in the man from heaven"?

No. He instead says, "Truly, truly, I say to you, unless you eat the flesh of the Son of man and drink his blood, you have no life in you; he who eats my flesh and drinks my blood has eternal life, and I will raise him up at the last day" (vv. 53-54). Jesus knows that they're taking him literally, but he doubles down, telling them that eating his flesh and drinking his blood is necessary for their salvation. And he doesn't stop there, adding that "my flesh is food indeed, and my blood is drink indeed" (v. 55). If that isn't enough, he then adds,

He who eats my flesh and drinks my blood abides in
me, and I in him. As the living Father sent me, and
I live because of the Father, so he who eats me will
live because of me. This is the bread which came
down from heaven, not such as the fathers ate and
died; he who eats this bread will live for ever (vv.
56-58).

In other words, Jesus has led his listeners *away from* taking
him simply to mean free food, or manna, or even belief in
him, and *into* taking him to mean that we must somehow
eat his flesh and drink his blood. And having led them into
this interpretation and doubled down on it, Jesus then triples
down, and quadruples down.

You need not take my word for it. The Protestant theologian F.F. Bruce says of the crowd's response in verse 52:

They did not suppose that he seriously implied cannibalism, yet that was the natural sense of his words.
It was an offensive way of speaking, they thought,
even if he was speaking figuratively. And if he was
speaking figuratively, they could not fathom what
the figurative sense of his words might be. Some had
one interpretation, some another, and a wordy strife
broke out among them. Is it too farfetched to see
in this wordy strife an anticipation of the perennial
controversies in which Christians have engaged over
the meaning of their Lord's words of institution,
"This is my body, which is for you" (1 Cor. 11:24)?[16]

Jesus' words seem to be literal, but it doesn't make sense
for him to be endorsing cannibalism. On the other hand, if

he's instead using a metaphor, it's not clear *what that metaphor means*, either to his original listeners or to modern Christians. Of course, the Eucharist solves this: Jesus isn't speaking merely metaphorically, but neither is he endorsing cannibalism.

Bruce points out that in responding to the people, "Jesus amplifies his contentious statement. The amplification was more offensive than the original statement." First, Jesus brings up that not only must we eat his flesh, but we must also drink his blood. Since the Law of Moses forbade drinking blood, "the idea of drinking the blood of the Son of Man was impossibly abhorrent." (Of course, even those of us who don't keep kosher would agree!) Second, Jesus' language about eating gets more graphic: the Greek text switches from *phagein*, which means simply "to eat," to *trōgein*, a "coarser word" meaning "'to munch' or 'to chew,'—used in classical Greek of animals eating."[17]

So with that in mind, let's go back to Bruce's earlier point: if this is all just a metaphor, what's it a metaphor *for?*

A common interpretation is that eating Christ's flesh and drinking his blood "means neither more nor less than believing in Christ."[18] But how is drinking blood a metaphor for belief? Certainly, there's a sense in which we can talk about feasting on God's word. In Matthew 4:4, Jesus quotes Deuteronomy 8:3 to prove that "man shall not live by bread alone, but by every word that proceeds from the mouth of God." But it's a far cry from that to using "gnaw my flesh and drink my blood" as a way of saying "believe in me." Indeed, the closest the Bible gets to using that kind of blood-drinking imagery is in Revelation 17:6, where the Whore of Babylon is depicted as "drunk with the blood of the saints and the blood of the martyrs of Jesus," as a way of saying that she *murders Christians.*

But there's another problem with taking this all as merely metaphorical: if John 6 is just Jesus using a convoluted metaphor to say "have faith," then it has nothing to do with the Lord's Supper at all. And that's exactly what many Protestant commentators claim: that Jesus' words in John 6 "were not spoken with any reference to the sacrament of the Lord's Supper."[19] According to this view, Jesus metaphorically calls his body bread in John 6, and a year later he metaphorically calls bread his body at the Last Supper, and these two moments are unrelated . . . even though they're both set at Passover, and even though "the verb rendered 'gave thanks' in [John 6] verse eleven is *eucharisteo*, from which we derive the term Eucharist ('thanksgiving'), commonly used of the Holy Communion."[20] It takes a lot of effort to miss the connection between these two events. *

A FIVE-PART TEST FOR YOUR EUCHARISTIC BELIEFS

How can you tell if you have the right understanding—the biblical interpretation, Jesus' interpretation—of the Eucharist? I'd suggest five things to look for: your beliefs should be *strange, sacrificial, serious, sacramental,* and *shocking.*

First, as we've already seen, the proper Christian understanding of the Eucharist must be *strange*, and hard to accept.

---

* Even after all of this discussion about John 6, there's one important dimension that we still haven't covered: what does Jesus mean in John 6:63 when he says that "it is the spirit that gives life, the flesh is of no avail; the words that I have spoken to you are spirit and life"? Does "flesh" mean "literal," and "spirit" mean "metaphorical"? Or to put it another way, is Jesus contradicting everything that he's just said about the salvific necessity of his flesh? Don't worry: we'll take a closer look at that verse, and how it has been misconstrued, a bit later on.

That's how it was initially received, and Jesus did nothing to dispel this impression. If he was trying to present an easy teaching and was just being misunderstood, why would he *not* clarify?

And this teaching is not just strange to the world, but even to Jesus' own followers. John tells us that after the Bread of Life discourse, "many of his disciples drew back and no longer went about with him" (John 6:66). These are people who *didn't* leave after Jesus "called God his Father, making himself equal with God" (5:18). Some people who are perfectly willing to embrace the divinity of Christ find his eucharistic teaching too extreme. And Jesus responds to this by challenging even the Twelve, "Will you also go away?" Simon Peter's response, "Lord, to whom shall we go? You have the words of eternal life" is one of tremendous faith, but Peter doesn't pretend that even he gets what Jesus means by these strange words (6:67-69). If your eucharistic beliefs aren't strange, even to other Christians, they're not the beliefs Jesus taught in John 6.

Second, the proper Christian understanding of the Eucharist must be *sacrificial.* St. Paul compares the eucharistic sacrifice to the pagan and Jewish sacrifices of his day, pointing out that "those who eat the [Jewish] sacrifices" become "partners in the altar" whereas those who eat the pagan sacrifices become "partners with demons" (1 Cor. 10:18-20). He draws a clear parallel between "the cup of the Lord" and "the cup of demons," as well as between "the table of the Lord" and "the table of demons." Read that again: he describes what's happening in the Eucharist by *comparing it with what takes place at demonic altars* (v. 21). If your understanding of the Eucharist *isn't* a sacrifice comparable to the fleshly sacrifices offered in the Temple in Jerusalem or in pagan rites, then you don't believe what Paul believed.

Third, the proper Christian understanding of the Eucharist must be *serious*. Paul recounts for the Corinthians the events of the Last Supper, which he says he "received from the Lord" (1 Cor. 11:23). Paul never met Jesus during his earthly ministry; it seems that what he's about to relate concerning the Eucharist he learned through a special revelation from him. If that's right, it speaks to just how seriously Jesus takes the Eucharist. He doesn't just leave it up to us to figure out how best to commemorate or honor or worship him.

And for those who *don't* take the Eucharist seriously? Paul warns that whoever "eats the bread or drinks the cup of the Lord in an unworthy manner will be guilty of profaning the body and blood of the Lord," since whoever "eats and drinks without discerning the body eats and drinks judgment upon himself" (vv. 28-29). He even adds that this is why many of his Corinthian readers "are weak and ill, and some have died" (v. 30).* If it wouldn't make sense to say that anyone approaching this mystery unworthily risks damning themselves, then you don't believe the same thing as Paul, and he received his views from Jesus.

Fourth, the proper Christian understanding of the Eucharist must be *sacramental*. In his commentary on John 6, the Evangelical biblical scholar D.A. Carson admits that the early Christians understood the Eucharist not merely as a

---

* It's hard to square this seriousness with a symbolic view of the Eucharist. After all, if the Eucharist were simply a symbol reminding us of Jesus' death and resurrection, Paul would be saying here, "If you don't find this symbolic reminder helpful, Jesus will send you to hell!"

symbol or as a reminder of Jesus' past action, but as a *sacrament*. And they believed the sacraments were capable of "conveying grace in and of themselves."[21] That is, they're not effective simply because we believe in them, or because they remind us of God, but because God is doing something miraculous through them. Carson points out that even St. Ignatius of Antioch "adopts a sacramentarian stance."[22] Why does this matter? Because Ignatius seems to have been a disciple of the apostle John, and he's writing around A.D. 107, only about seven years after the death of the apostle. If *anyone* can shed light on what John 6 means, surely it would be one of John's own students.

And what's more, we don't find any evidence of some kind of early Christian outcry against this teaching—of people telling Ignatius that he's betraying the theology of John and the other apostles. In fact, as we'll see later, Ignatius *assumes* that, in the year 107, a faithful Christian is someone who takes a sacramental view of the Eucharist. If your beliefs about the Eucharist *aren't* sacramental, then they're not compatible with the beliefs of those who knew the apostolic preaching and teaching way better than we do.

Fifth and finally, the proper Christian understanding of the Eucharist must be *shocking*. The crowd didn't just find the teaching hard, or strange—they found it repulsive, because they mistook it for cannibalism. And that didn't stop with John 6. One of the oldest arguments against Christianity from the ancient world is that Christians were engaged in ritual cannibalism,[23] a misconception that seems to have stemmed from misunderstanding the Eucharist. So if your beliefs about the Eucharist *aren't* liable to being misunderstood as cannibalism, then they're not the beliefs held by the earliest Christians.

If we get this right—if we arrive at a view of the Eucharist that's strange, sacrificial, serious, sacramental, and shocking—more than just the Last Supper or John 6 will make more sense. Suddenly, other surprising and seemingly-unrelated parts of the faith will "click" in a new and meaningful way. Like what? Well, that's what the rest of the book is about. But let's start with the *covenant* heart of Christianity.

2

The Key to
CHRISTIANITY

What are the Old and New Testament? That might seem like an easy question to answer. These are two collections of inspired books: the Old Testament books prophesying about the coming of the Messiah, and the New Testament books describing what it was like when Jesus the Messiah finally came.

But nowhere in the Bible are the biblical books described as the "Old Testament" or the "New Testament" (or, for that matter, as the "Bible"). Instead, we find Jesus calling the Old Testament books the "scriptures" (Matt. 21:42, 22:29, etc.), "the law and the prophets" (Matt. 5:17; 7:12; 22:40; Luke 16:16), "the prophets and the law" (Matt. 11:13), and, in one instance, "the law of Moses and the prophets and the psalms" (Luke 24:44).[24] Similarly, the collection of books we now call "the New Testament" are never called by that name within those books.

In fact, the phrase *new testament* didn't originally refer to books at all. The word *testament* comes from the Latin *testamentum,* which can also be translated as "covenant."[25] So, "new testament" at least roughly means "new covenant."

Why, then, did the early Christians choose to call the parts of the Bible the "Old Testament" and the "New Testament"? In the words of Cardinal Joseph Ratzinger, the future Pope Benedict XVI, they wanted to bring to light "the central theme of Scripture itself, thus giving a key to the whole of it," since the "very word 'testament' is, in a way, an attempt to utter the 'essence of Christianity' in a single, summary, expression."[26] That is, they used the word because they understood the contents of Scripture as a story about God's *covenantal* relationship(s) with his people.

The Old Testament scholar Victor H. Matthews argues that "the single most overriding theme in the Old Testament is covenant. From this all-encompassing idea flows much of the narrative, wisdom, prophecy, and spirituality of the Bible."[27] Likewise, the story of the New Testament is about how God, through Jesus, created a new covenant with his people.

THE COVENANTAL HEART
OF CHRISTIANITY

This means that you cannot properly understand Christianity without understanding the new covenant. This is a point upon which Catholics and many[28] Protestants agree. The nineteenth-century Baptist preacher Charles Spurgeon lamented that "in some congregations people never hear the word 'covenant' and yet he that understands the two covenants has the key of theology! The covenants are the diamond hinges on which the golden doors of Grace are made to turn."[29] Calvinist theologian J.I. Packer likewise describes what he calls "the life-embracing bedrock reality of the covenant relationship between the Creator and Christians."[30] Scott Hahn makes a similar point:

> The covenant *defines* religion for Christians and Jews. We cannot discern God's design or his will if we do not meditate upon his covenant. . . . The covenant, then, is the principle that unites the New Testament with the Old, the scriptures with tradition, and each of the various branches of theology with all the others. The covenant does more than bridge the gaps between these elements; it fills in the gaps, so that biblical scholarship, dogmatic theology, and magisterial authority all stand on common ground—solid ground.[31]

But why is covenantal theology so important? Isn't Christianity about relationship? Exactly.

In the words of Pope Benedict XVI, Christianity "is not the result of an ethical choice or a lofty idea, but the encounter with an event, a person, which gives life a new horizon and a decisive direction" (*Deus Caritas Est* 1). To put is slightly differently, Christianity (like Judaism before it) is all about two sets of relationships: our relationship with God and our relationship with our neighbors.

You don't have to take my word for it. Jesus says as much himself:

> But when the Pharisees heard that [Jesus] had silenced the Sadducees, they came together. And one of them, a lawyer, asked him a question, to test him. "Teacher, which is the great commandment in the

law?" And he said to him, "You shall love the Lord
your God with all your heart, and with all your soul,
and with all your mind. This is the great and first
commandment. And a second is like it, You shall
love your neighbor as yourself. On these two commandments depend all the law and the prophets"
(Matt. 22:34–40).

So what do covenants and relationships have to do with
one another? As Baptist theologians Peter Gentry and Stephen Wellum put it, "the question of relationships is handled in the Bible by one concept, one word: covenant. And
the question of an overall plan is handled by the sequence of
significant covenants."[32]

Gert Kwakkel, a professor of the Old Testament, explains
that the word for *covenant* in Hebrew, *berith*, means "the
agreement or convention that is at the base of a relationship
or regulates it."[33] But why does our love of God (or our love
of neighbor, for that matter) need "regulation" in the first
place? Why not just have relationship instead of religion?

For starters, the Bible rejects this false dichotomy between
relationship and religion. Christianity is explicitly relational,
but it's also explicitly a religion (see 1 Tim. 3:16; James 1:27).
Here, it helps to consider the image of covenant relationship
used throughout Scripture: that of the Bridegroom and the
bride. Why should couples bother with getting married in
the first place? Isn't love enough? Or why not simply follow
our sexual desires, without worrying so much about rules?

But the mature (and Christian) response to this is that
a relationship needs more than passion or good feelings to
survive. It needs structure and form—not to stifle it, but to
harness and direct it. (In the words of Ray Ortlund, "Sex

is like fire. In the fireplace, it keeps us warm. Outside the fireplace, it burns the house down."[34])

To contain the fire: that's why marriage exists, and it's also why religion exists. Man has a desire to serve God, and some kind of desire to serve his fellow men. But outside of the covenantal fireplace, these well-meaning impulses can burn down humanity's household through sectarian warfare and disastrous utopian schemes. Without some clear sense of how to serve (and *not* to serve) God and neighbor, we're in a lot of trouble.

Ratzinger argues that the idea of covenant not only joins relationship with religion—it reveals something about God's nature:

> When we say that man is the image of God, it means that he is a being designed for relationship; it means that, in and through all his relationships, he seeks that relation which is the ground of his existence. In this context, covenant would be the response to man's imaging of God; it would show us who we are and who God is. And for God, since he is entirely relationship, covenant would not be something external in history, apart from his being, but the manifestation of his self, the "radiance of his countenance."[35]

God reveals himself as a Trinity, three divine Persons in a relationship of ordered charity with one another. This outpouring of love gives rise to the creation of the universe, and of ourselves. No idea gets more central—to Christianity, to theology, to our understanding of reality—than the covenant.

THE EUCHARISTIC HEART
OF THE COVENANT

But just as you cannot properly understand Christianity without understanding the new covenant, you cannot properly understand the new covenant without understanding the Eucharist. And it's here that those brilliant Protestant theologians fall short. Take Packer, for instance. He argues that "God's covenant of grace in Scripture is one of those things that are too big to be easily seen, particularly when one's mind is programmed to look at something smaller."[36] He gives the example of looking for "a particular Polynesian island" on a map of the Pacific, and (with eyes attuned to the small printed names of each island) overlooking the massive letters "PACIFIC OCEAN."

In Packer's way of thinking, realities like "God's promises," "circumcision, passover, baptism, the Lord's Supper," and so forth, are all like these small "islands" within the ocean of covenantal theology, and the danger is that we focus on these things "without noticing that these relational realities are all covenantal in their very essence."[37] Packer is right to see the enormous significance of covenant, but he's wrong to see "the Lord's Supper" as just a tiny island within that vast sea.

Indeed, this is in stark contrast to the way Jesus describes the covenant. The Bible only records one moment in which Jesus explicitly spoke of the "new covenant" or covenants at all. That moment is at the Last Supper. Here's how Matthew records the moment:

> Now as they were eating, Jesus took bread, and
> blessed, and broke it, and gave it to the disciples and

said, "Take, eat; this is my body." And he took a cup, and when he had given thanks he gave it to them, saying, "Drink of it, all of you; for this is my blood of the covenant, which is poured out for many for the forgiveness of sins. I tell you I shall not drink again of this fruit of the vine until that day when I drink it new with you in my Father's kingdom" (Matt. 26:26-29).

Mark's description closely matches Matthew's, with Jesus describing the contents of the chalice as "my blood of the covenant" (Mark 14:24). Paul records Jesus' words as "this cup is the new covenant in my blood" (1 Cor. 11:25), while Luke has "this cup which is poured out for you is the new covenant in my blood" (Luke 22:20).

Together, a clear picture emerges: at the Last Supper, Jesus claimed that the contents of the eucharistic chalice he offered were (1) the blood of the covenant, (2) the blood that he was to pour out on the cross the following day for the forgiveness of sins, and (3) the inauguration of the new covenant. To use Packer's imagery, it's as if Jesus help up the chalice of his blood and said, "Here it is, the PACIFIC OCEAN."

EUCHARISTIC + COVENANTAL CHRISTIANITY

So, the heart of Christianity is a covenant, and the center of that covenant is the Eucharist, which is really Jesus. But what would it look like to understand Christianity in a covenantal and eucharistic way? As we've seen, covenants are "inherently relational."[38] This helps to clarify the difference between covenants and other types of contractual relationships. As Hahn explains,

> Contracts usually exchange property, goods, and services. But covenants exchange persons. Contracts set the terms for a business transaction. But covenants create a family bond. Every covenant is based upon a contract, since all interpersonal relationships involve some sharing of property and obligations of service. Still, a covenant extends far beyond the limits of any contract. When people enter into a covenant, they say "I am yours, and you are mine." Thus, marriage is a covenant, and adoption is a covenant.[39]

When we think about contracts, we think in terms of *justice*: did each party do what it agreed to do? But when we think about covenants, we go beyond this, asking instead about *fidelity* and even *love*.[40] Understanding the relational dimension of a covenant is critical, or else we'll be stuck thinking about Christianity in transactional, legal terms, with God as the Judge but not the Father, and with Christ as the Ransom but not the Bridegroom.

Hahn asserts that "far more than the new covenant being made in a courtroom, it was fashioned by God in a family room."[41] We might go even further: *contract* invokes the image of a courtroom, but *covenant*, particularly when connected with the marital imagery used of Christ's relationship with the Church, is more likely to invoke the image of a bedroom. If that description of divine-human communion seems too risqué, it's worth remembering that the traditional way that both Jewish and Christian readers have understood the seemingly erotic language of the Song of

Songs is as an allegory for God's covenantal relationship with his people.[42]

This is an important shift away from the moralism and legalism into which Christians can easily fall. Think of it this way: imagine explaining marriage to someone who had never heard of it before. One explanation would be to start with the *no's*—all of those restrictions that come with marriage. You lose control of your free time, your personal finances, your ability to date different people, and so on. But beginning that way would create a distorted image of marriage, and the person would reasonably ask, "Why in the world would anyone sign up for this?" To make sense of marriage—or Christianity—you have to start with understanding it as a loving *yes*: a yes so intense that you freely choose to be bound to someone else forever. That doesn't deny those no's, but it helps to make sense of them and to put them in their proper place.

Christianity isn't about a contract in which, if we check all of the boxes, God will consent to love us. Christianity is a covenantal relationship with the God who already loves us, and the beating heart of that covenant is in the Eucharist. If we want to know how to enter into the deepest bonds of communion with God possible on this earth, or if we want to know how to properly worship God, or if we want to understand Jesus' incarnation or the dignity of our own body, or if we want to know how to live like a saint, or if we want to know God's plan for our redemption . . . in each case, the answer is found right there, in the Eucharist. If you don't see how yet, don't worry. We'll unpack each of these ideas in due time.

But before we do, I want to address an idea closely related to covenant: *blood sacrifice*. After all, if Protestant readers fail to see the importance of the Eucharist for each of the areas I've just mentioned, that's perfectly understandable. After all, if you're inclined to think of Jesus' words and actions at the Last Supper as merely symbolic, or inaugurating some kind of merely "spiritual presence," then it's difficult to see why Jesus' words at the Last Supper would be central.

Jesus plainly describes the Last Supper as the institution of the new covenant. But as we're about to see, that only makes sense if he's holding a chalice of his own blood when he says that. If that still sounds crazy to you, read on, because we're going to need to unpack the controversial idea of blood sacrifice in the Bible, as well as its particular role in establishing biblical covenants.

3

The Key to the
BLOODY CROSS

When Jesus lifts the chalice at the Last Supper, he instructs the apostles, "Drink of it, all of you; for this is my blood of the covenant, which is poured out for many for the forgiveness of sins" (Matt. 26:27-28). So not only is the Eucharist described as Christ's blood, but this blood is "poured out for many." That is, the idea of covenant is intimately linked with the idea of blood sacrifice.

Daniel L. Smith explains a covenant as "a binding agreement between two or more parties. In the ancient Near Eastern world, this sort of binding agreement was often solemnized through blood sacrifice."[43] Of course, this feature of covenants, and of sacrifices more broadly, is scandalous to modern ears. In *An Atheist in the Choir Loft*, Robert Simpson says that his "major issue with Christianity" is "the idea of blood sacrifices to appease or make amends with gods." In Simpson's words,

> The Israelite people had a culture that was quite
> bloodthirsty. Killing and bloodletting was viewed

by them as a necessary part of showing their loy-
alty to their god. I think their belief in the need for
blood offerings was as misguided as that of the May-
ans' idea of sacrificing people for their god.[44]

Simpson is hardly alone in this view of Israel's history.
Christopher Hitchens, a major figure of the "New Athe-
ism," blamed the 1994 Cave of the Patriarchs massacre (an
act of anti-Muslim terrorism committed by a radical Jewish doctor) on Old Testament animal sacrifice, arguing that
"the curse of Abraham continues to poison Hebron, but the
religious warrant for blood sacrifice poisons our entire civilization."[45] It's not only unbelievers who find these depic-
tions of God demanding animal sacrifice troubling: plenty
of Jewish and Christian readers struggle to make sense of
these Old Testament passages, as well.

But making sense of these passages is critical for understanding Jesus' death on the cross and the whole Christian
notion of the "atonement." Sam Harris, another prominent
atheist, argues that "humanity has had a long fascination
with blood sacrifice," and that "the notion that Jesus Christ
died for our sins and that his death constitutes a successful
propitiation of a 'loving' God is a direct and undisguised
inheritance of the superstitious bloodletting that has plagued
bewildered people throughout history."[46] Harris is wrong to
write this all off as ancient superstition, but he's right to see
Jesus' death as having something to do with that history of
Israelite animal sacrifices.

Whether we're talking about animal sacrifice in the Old
Testament or the sacrifice of Jesus Christ in the New, we can
ask the same question: are these sacrifices simply evidence

of a superstitious and a violent people or a bloodthirsty god? Or is there something else going on?

Broadly speaking, there are two types of sacrifices. The first is what we might call an "unwilling sacrifice," as was practiced in many pagan religions in Europe, Asia, and the Americas. Among the most notorious practitioners were the Aztecs. Addressing his people, the Aztec leader Cuauhtlequetzqui once announced, "Know, O my children, that this night our god Huitzilopochtli appeared to me. Remember, on our arrival in this valley . . . Our enemies drove us from that region, but Huitzilopochtli commanded us to kill Copil and this we did, taking out his heart. And standing in the place where the god commanded, I threw the heart into the reeds: it fell upon a rock."[47] At Huitzilopochtli's insistence, the Aztecs build the city of Tenochtitlan (modern-day Mexico City) at the site where Cuauhtlequetzqui threw Copil's heart.

What's striking here is that there's no hero to this story. That's because, in an unwilling sacrifice, the victim has no real agency. We can feel pity for Copil, but not admiration.

And this, unfortunately, is the way even many Christians describe Jesus' sacrifice on the cross. Many Protestant preachers today argue that God the Father poured out his wrath upon Jesus on Good Friday.[48] In *The Murder of Jesus*, John MacArthur writes that Jesus "received the very same outpouring of divine wrath in all its fury that *we* deserved for our sin," a punishment "so severe that a mortal could spend all eternity in the torments of hell, and still he would not have begun to exhaust the divine wrath that was heaped on Christ at the cross."[49]

And in this view of the cross, God the Father *does* seem

to be a murderer. John Piper said that "God the Father lifted his knife over the chest of his own Son, Jesus," while R.C. Sproul says that "God ordained the murder of Jesus."[50] According to Sproul, it is "as if Jesus heard the words 'God damn you.' Because that's what it meant to be cursed, to be damned, to be under the anathema of a Father."[51] This idea that God the Father murders and then damns God the Son goes back to the Protestant Reformer John Calvin, who argued that "there is nothing strange in its being said that [Christ] descended to hell,* seeing he endured the death which is inflicted on the wicked by an angry God."[52] It's easy to see why atheists (and indeed, believers) might be scandalized by this idea of the cross, since it seems to turn Jesus into Copil, and God the Father into bloodthirsty Huitzilopochtli.

But this isn't how the Bible presents the cross. Jesus says that "for this reason the Father loves me, because I lay down my life, that I may take it again" (John 10:17). Jesus isn't a helpless victim, like Copil. Instead, he says, "No one takes [my life] from me, but I lay it down of my own accord. I have power to lay it down, and I have power to take it again; this charge I have received from my Father" (v. 18). And the Father responds to Jesus' willing sacrifice not with

---

* In traditional Christian theology, Christ's descent into hell is celebrated as his *triumph*, not his *punishment*. St. Peter says that Jesus "went and preached to the spirits in prison, who formerly did not obey, when God's patience waited in the days of Noah" (1 Pet. 3:19-20), and an ancient homily (anonymous, but ascribed to St. Epiphanius) says that Christ "goes to seek out our first parent like a lost sheep; he wishes to visit those who sit in darkness and in the shadow of death. He goes to free the prisoner Adam and his fellow-prisoner Eve from their pains, he who is God, and Adam's son. The Lord goes in to them holding his victorious weapon, his cross."

bloodthirstiness or wrath or by damning his only-begotten Son, but with love.

Understanding the cross as a *willing* sacrifice changes everything. In 2012, a gunman entered a sold-out movie theater in Aurora, Colorado, indiscriminating firing into the crowd. Twelve people were killed, and another fifty-eight were wounded. Among the slain was Alexander "Alex" Teves, a twenty-four-year-old on a date with his girlfriend. When the shooting began, Teves pulled his girlfriend to the floor and covered her with his own body, taking a bullet to the forehead.[53]

Teves was not alone in his heroism that night: Matthew "Matt" McQuinn, Jon Blunk, and U.S. Navy Petty Officer Third Class John Larimer, all in their twenties, died shielding their girlfriends at the cost of their own lives.[54] Larimer's girlfriend would later describe how "John immediately and instinctively covered me and brought me to the ground in order to protect me from any danger. Moments later, John knowingly shielded me from a spray of gunshots. It was then I believe John was hit with a bullet that would have very possibly struck me. I feel very strongly that I was saved by John and his ultimate kindness."[55] In the words of Colorado's then-governor John Hickenlooper, "heroism isn't strong enough a word" to describe the self-sacrificial deaths of these four young men.[56] And indeed, there *is* a stronger word to describe what these four men embodied: love.

The meaning of an unwilling sacrifice is *violence*: the strong destroy the weak. But the meaning of a willing sacrifice is *love*: you love someone or something more than your own life. Or in the words of Jesus of Nazareth, "Greater love has no man than this, that a man lay down his life for his friends" (John 15:13). Another difference is that, in a willing sacrifice, the priest (that is, the one offering the sacrifice) *is the victim*. Those four men offered their lives out of love. And Jesus offered his own life for us. That's what holding up his body and blood at the Last Supper means: he's presenting himself, willingly, to be sacrificed out of love for us. Paul puts it like this:

> While we were yet helpless, at the right time Christ died for the ungodly. Why, one will hardly die for a righteous man—though perhaps for a good man one will dare even to die. But God shows his love for us in that while we were yet sinners Christ died for us (Rom. 5:6-8).

Christ isn't an unwilling victim; he's the priest of the sacrifice. And God the Father isn't an unjust judge who damns the innocent (Jesus) so he can let the guilty (us) go free. Paul teaches that the cross is an expression, not of divine wrath, but of *God's love for us*.

This helps us to make sense of how Jesus' death on the cross "works."* As St. Thomas Aquinas explains, you properly atone for an offense if you offer "something which the offended one loves equally, or even more than he detested the offense."[57] When my daughter takes a toy from her younger brother, she's quick to offer him a different toy. If he likes the new toy better, crisis averted: atonement has been achieved.

---

* Perhaps more accurately, this explains *one way* that the cross works. Aquinas explores the "efficiency" of the cross from several angles: merit, atonement, sacrifice, redemption, atonement, and satisfaction. So this is an important part of the story, but not the full story of the cross.

So how does Jesus offer the Father atonement? Aquinas says that "by suffering out of love and obedience, Christ gave more to God than was required to compensate for the offense of the whole human race."[58] In other words, the cross isn't about God being bloodthirsty. It's about Jesus' selfless love on the cross being *bigger than sin:* greater than all of the sins of the entire human race for all time. Good Friday isn't a story about divine violence but divine love.

CUTTING (AND BINDING) A COVENANT

This twofold shift—understanding Christ's sacrifice as about love instead of violence, and putting it in the context of his creating a new covenant at the Last Supper—also makes sense of the bloody nature of the cross. The Hebrew term for forming a covenant, *likhrot brit,* literally means "to cut a covenant." Why is a covenant said to be "cut"? The Reformed theologian Max Stackhouse argues that "the usage of 'cut' derives from a ritual meal—one that sees covenant-making in the context of a sacrificial rite that involves the presence or witness of God and establishes a system of justice by stipulating a framework of duties and rights."[59]

Perhaps the most interesting writer on this subject is the political scientist Daniel Elazar, who wrote a four-volume work on the idea of covenant. Elazar, an observant Jew and an expert on Jewish history, devotes the first of those four volumes to exploring "Covenant and Polity in Biblical Israel." Why so much focus here? Because, as Elazar explains, "the entire worldview of the Bible and consequently the essential outlook of all biblically rooted traditions is built around the covenant idea."[60] According to Elazar, there are several ways that a covenant could be "cut":

Sealing a covenant involves some ritual act. In the Bible, sacrifice is the common ritual but there also were the common meal and oath. Thus, Moses, Aaron, Aaron's sons, and the seventy elders of Israel representing the entire people, shared a common meal upon completion of the Sinai covenant (cf. Exod. 24:1-12). Other forms include drinking together, gift-giving, exchange of names, sacrifices, kissing, and hand-shaking. Indeed, so much so that one way to forbid establishing a covenantal relationship was to forbid eating together. The idea of the common meal becomes an important ritual in both Judaism and Christianity, with the latter emphasizing the taking of food as the means of organically linking with the Savior.[61]

Elazar mentioned Exodus 24, which we'll take a closer look at shortly. For now, it's important to recognize that a covenant is "cut" with a ritual act that is (1) communal, (2) often involving blood, and (3) often taking the form of a shared ritual meal. Elazar even seems to nod to a fact that many Christians don't realize: that the Last Supper was all three of these.

The biblical imagery for covenant-formation involves two seemingly-opposite sets of biblical images here: "cutting" and "binding." In Genesis 17, God says to Abraham, "This is my covenant, which you shall keep, between me and you and your descendants after you: Every male among you shall be circumcised . . . So shall my covenant be in your flesh an everlasting covenant" (vv. 10, 13). This "cutting" of the first covenant was painfully literal! But the covenant was also "binding." Elazar argues that we see this with

Abraham's son Isaac, the first son to be born in the covenant of circumcision. The Hebrew term for Abraham's near sacrifice of Isaac in Genesis 22 is translated as the "binding of Isaac," a phrase with rich covenantal significance:

> Binding is, of course, an element of covenanting and the choice of that term to describe this critical, poignant, and moving event is another reflection of the pervasiveness of covenantal thinking in the Bible and Israel in all its generations. Isaac is the first full *ben brit*, son of the covenant; he is circumcised—cut—according to God's command and then he is bound over to God.[62]

We see these two dimensions of cutting and binding throughout the Old Testament, particularly in a striking passage from Exodus 24.

THE BLOOD OF THE COVENANT(S)

Hebrews 9 pinpoints the ratification of the Old Covenant to a specific moment in the book of Exodus, in which Moses, having received the words of the covenant, reads them to the people while splashing both the altar *and the people* with basins full of blood. Here's how Exodus 24 describes that moment:

> And he [Moses] rose early in the morning, and built an altar at the foot of the mountain, and twelve pillars, according to the twelve tribes of Israel. And he sent young men of the people of Israel, who offered burnt offerings and sacrificed peace offerings

of oxen to the Lord. And Moses took half of the blood and put it in basins, and half of the blood he threw against the altar. Then he took the book of the covenant, and read it in the hearing of the people; and they said, "All that the Lord has spoken we will do, and we will be obedient." And Moses took the blood and threw it upon the people, and said, "Behold the blood of the covenant which the Lord has made with you in accordance with all these words" (vv. 4b-8).

In his book *Blood Ritual in the Hebrew Bible,* Emory's William K. Gilders points out that since the Hebrew verb used here "indicates a flinging motion, we may envisage Moses standing before the people, perhaps elevated above them, and tossing blood out of a vessel of some sort—perhaps the 'bowls' in which it was stored, if these could be picked up and handled—so that it fell down on the people. This is, to say the least, a striking ritual act."[63]

But what does this "striking ritual act" mean? There's a negative interpretation of the passage: that the blood is a kind of "blood curse" or "a warning that their blood will be spilled if they break the covenant."[64] This is the interpretation that Harris and Hitchens and so many others assume: that sacrifices are bloody because God is bloodthirsty, or because superstitious ancients believed in bloodthirsty gods. But if that's what's meant, why would Moses first sprinkle the altar? Instead, the Old Testament scholar G. Henton Davies argues that with the sprinkling of blood first on the altar (representing God) and then on the people, the two parties are united as one in a sacramental union:

Both partners, divine and human, are joined and united so far as the matter in hand is concerned—the giving and accepting of the words of the Lord—in the blood of the animals which have been slaughtered. Whereas in the giving and accepting of the law the Lord and people stand over against each other as contracting partners, in the blood ritual they are organically related and become united. This is the sacramental at-one-ment of the covenant relationship.[65]

One thing that may help us to understand this is to think of the way that young boys will sometimes become "blood brothers" with their close friends by nicking their hands enough to draw blood and then shaking hands to mingle the blood together. It's critical for this childhood ritual that there be blood: simply pantomiming cutting your hand wouldn't be enough. But the blood isn't a threat: it's an expression of the depth of their unity. Cutting and binding are not opposite actions, but two halves of a covenantal sealing. Gilders and Davies argue that something like this is happening here, with the sacrificial, sacramental blood uniting God and the people as one (the literal root meaning of *atonement*).

This is also the explanation given in Leviticus itself: "For the life of the flesh is in the blood; and I have given it for you upon the altar to make atonement for your souls; for it is the blood that makes atonement, by reason of the life" (Lev. 17:11).

In John 6, Jesus says that "unless you eat the flesh of the Son of man and drink his blood, you have no life in you," and some Protestants have pointed to this part of

Leviticus to argue that "only a figurative interpretation of the Last Supper is in harmony with the whole counsel of God," since "God commanded mankind to abstain from blood."[66] But the whole point in Leviticus is that drinking the blood of an animal was forbidden because it would be a kind of *communion with that animal*. When we receive the blood of Christ, we're communing not with a creature but with God.*

Understanding this blood of the first covenant as a covenantal sharing in life also makes sense of what happens next to Moses and the others:

> Then Moses and Aaron, Nadab, and Abihu, and seventy of the elders of Israel went up, and they saw the God of Israel; and there was under his feet as it were a pavement of sapphire stone, like the very heaven for clearness. And he did not lay his hand on the chief men of the people of Israel; they beheld God, and ate and drank (Exod. 24:9-11).

So God and the people being united in blood is linked in Exodus 24 to this mysterious heavenly banquet in which the leaders of Israel "beheld God, and ate and drank." The divine-human union that begins on earth, with God coming to the people, then enters a new phase, with the people

---

* There's no contradiction between Jesus' teaching on drinking his blood and the Mosaic Law's prohibition of the drinking of animal blood. In his letters, Paul uses the same verse from Genesis (2:23, about the man and woman becoming one flesh) both to show why fornication with prostitutes is wrong (1 Cor. 6:16) and why marital relations are right (Eph. 5:29-31). Likewise, if you understand what Leviticus 17 says about communion in the blood, it should be clear both why communing with animals is wrong (and forbidden under the Mosaic Law) whereas communing with God is good.

going to God. As Brant Pitre points out, "although the sacrificial liturgy begins on earth, it climaxes with a heavenly banquet."[67]

So the inauguration of the first covenant involved a rite that was communal, involved blood, and culminated in a shared ritual meal, the three elements Elazar said we would find. Perhaps the parallels between this and the institution of the Eucharist at the Last Supper are already clear. But in case they're not, here's how Hebrews 9:18-22 makes the connection:

> Hence even the first covenant was not ratified without blood. For when every commandment of the law had been declared by Moses to all the people, he took the blood of calves and goats, with water and scarlet wool and hyssop, and sprinkled both the book itself and all the people, saying, "This is the blood of the covenant which God commanded you." And in the same way he sprinkled with the blood both the tent and all the vessels used in worship. Indeed, under the law almost everything is purified with blood, and without the shedding of blood there is no forgiveness of sins.

Notice the way that the inspired author says that "even" the first covenant needed blood to be ratified, taking it for granted that the *new* covenant was also ratified in this way. The ratification of the first covenant is tied to two moments. First, the author mentions Moses "sprinkling" the blood on the book of the Law, the people, the tent of meeting, and the vessels used in worship. That clearly prefigures the cross. Hebrews points us to "Jesus, the mediator of a new covenant, and to the sprinkled blood that speaks more graciously than the blood of Abel" (Heb. 12:24). So the blood of the new covenant is Jesus' own blood, and it is sacrificially and ritually "sprinkled" when it is poured out on Calvary on Good Friday.

But Hebrews also connects the ratification of the new covenant with Moses, saying, "This is the blood of the covenant which God commanded you." Where's the parallel in the new covenant? It's clearly the Last Supper, when Jesus says, "This cup which is poured out for you is the new covenant in my blood" (Luke 22:20).

In the New Testament narrative, these two moments are inseparably connected, just as Moses' declaration is inseparable from his sprinkling the blood and from the heavenly banquet that follows. This is why it matters that the Eucharist really is the body and blood of Jesus and not just a symbol or a "spiritual presence." After all, if Jesus *isn't* holding a chalice with his blood in it at the Last Supper, then the new covenant was ratified without blood, and the argument of Hebrews 9 no longer makes sense.

THE PASSOVER AND THE EUCHARIST

There's one more sacrifice that we need to talk about if we're going to understand the meaning of Jesus' sacrifice, and that's what Scripture calls "the sacrifice of the Lord's passover" (Exod. 12:27). After all, Paul says that "Christ, our paschal lamb, has been sacrificed" (1 Cor. 5:7), suggesting that it's *this* particular sacrifice that he's using to understand what Jesus has done for us.

The Passover sacrifice consists of two parts. On the fourteenth day of the month of Nisan, "the whole assembly of the congregation of Israel shall kill their lambs" (Exod. 12:7). This killing of the lambs is what the apostle John calls "the day of Preparation of the Passover" (John 19:14). That is, this isn't the complete sacrifice. As strange as this may sound to us today, it wasn't enough for the Passover lamb to be slaughtered. It had to also be eaten. And so the Passover itself began on the *fifteenth* day of Nisan, when "they shall eat the flesh that night, roasted," and being sure to "let none of it remain until the morning" (Exod. 12:8, 10). These two halves—the slaying of the lamb and the eating of the lamb—make up one sacrifice, not two. The Bible uses "the passover sacrifice" to refer both to the killing and the eating (Deut. 16:2, 6).

Critics of the sacrifice of the Mass, both during the Reformation and today, will often point to a particular verse from Hebrews that talks about how Jesus Christ, unlike the Jewish high priest, has no need "to offer sacrifices daily, first for his own sins and then for those of the people; he did this once for all when he offered up himself" (Heb. 7:27). Isn't the Mass *re-sacrificing* Christ?

No, just as the Passover meal wasn't "re-sacrificing" the lamb slain on Preparation Day.

This Preparation Day, the killing of the paschal lamb, foreshadowed Good Friday. It's not a coincidence that John calls Good Friday "the day of Preparation of the Passover" –that is, Preparation Day. And that happened once for all on Calvary, never to be repeated. But the Passover meal was a foreshadowing of something else: the Last Supper, and every subsequent Mass throughout history.* Jesus connects these two moments repeatedly, saying at the Last Supper, "I have earnestly desired to eat this passover with you before I suffer" (Luke 22:15). And strikingly, even though Luke had earlier described Preparation Day as "the day of Unleavened Bread, on which the passover lamb had to be sacrificed," none of the four Gospels mentions lamb at this Passover . . . even though that was the centerpiece of the sacrificial meal. The meaning is clear: Christ is instituting a *new* Passover, in which he himself is the meal.

WHAT WAS IN THE CHALICE?

To sum up, there are a few reasons why a proper under-standing of Old Testament sacrifices and covenant-making help us to understand the Eucharist. When Moses told the people to "behold the blood of the covenant," he was show-ing them real blood. If Jesus at the Last Supper is just hold-ing up a glass of wine (or grape juice) that vaguely looks like blood, then the new rite is inferior to the old one. And what's more, this wouldn't be a valid new covenant, since (as we saw) blood was required.

Perhaps the best way I can describe it to Protestant readers

---

* After all, the blood of Christ has to be applied to our lives. Many Protes-tants realize this: if you ask them when they got saved, they'll often point to either their baptism or a moment of conversion or some other meaning-ful moment in their own lifetime. I've never heard anyone answer, "I got saved on Good Friday, centuries before my birth" because they realize that the victory Jesus won for us on the cross still has to be applied to each of the redeemed. John says that "the blood of Jesus his Son cleanses us from all sin" (1 John 1:7); and notice that he uses the present tense. He doesn't say that Jesus cleansed us once for all. No, the blood of Jesus is being continu-ously made present in our own lives.

is to ask, "How would you respond to those who thought that what appeared to be Jesus' bloody death on the cross was really just a symbol?" The Quran, for instance, lambasts the Jews "for their saying: We have killed the Messiah, Jesus, son of Mary, the messenger of Allah," when in fact "they did not kill him, nor did they cause his death on the cross, but he was made to appear as such."[68] From these and similar remarks, most Muslims have concluded that God made someone else[69] look like Jesus and let that person be murdered in Jesus' place, a sort of inverted substitutionary atonement. From a Christian perspective, would you consider this "just as good"?

Muslims consider Jesus a prophet, and I think the Quran's account is meant to be a vindication of God's goodness and power: that he would never let one of his prophets be murdered. But of course, it's precisely the other way around. Jesus' death on the cross is a tremendous testimony of God's love for us (that "God so loved the world that he gave his only Son, that whoever believes in him should not perish but have eternal life," in the words of John 3:16), as well as Jesus' own love for us ("Greater love has no man than this, that a man lay down his life for his friends," as he says in John 15:13).

To deny that it's really Jesus on the cross is to empty the cross of its meaning and power. Likewise, to deny that it's really Jesus in the Eucharist is to empty the Eucharist of its meaning and power. Jesus Christ offers *himself* at the Last Supper, and in every Mass since. That's why it matters.

4

The Key to Christ's
BODY
(and Our Own)

The second-century bishop St. Irenaeus of Lyons tells the story of how "John, the disciple of the Lord, going to bathe at Ephesus, and perceiving Cerinthus within, rushed out of the bath-house without bathing, exclaiming, 'Let us fly, lest even the bath-house fall down, because Cerinthus, the enemy of the truth, is within.'"[70]

So who was this Cerinthus, and what was it about him that could inspire such a strong reaction from the Beloved Disciple? And more to the point, how was the Eucharist critical to defeating the heretical theology of Cerinthus and his followers?

THE GNOSTIC WAR ON THE BODY

Cerinthus is considered a leader in one of the first major heresies Christianity ever had to face: Gnosticism.[71] Although

Gnostic is an umbrella term for several similar belief systems, there are a few major ideas upon which all Gnostics were agreed. Gnostics viewed matter (and particularly the body) as evil: a sort of "prison" or "tomb" entrapping the divine soul.[72] They claimed that Jesus had revealed to an elect few his "secret teachings," and that this special knowledge (*gnosis*) enabled the Gnostics to be liberated from the evil world of matter and the flesh into the world of pure spirit.

There are two closely related ideas at the heart of Gnosticism: (1) I am my soul, not my body; and (2) salvation involves my (good) soul being freed from my (evil) body.

But this *isn't* what Christians have historically believed. As the *Catechism of the Catholic Church* (CCC) puts it, the Christian position is that "man, though made of body and soul, is a unity" (382). You are not "just" your body or "just" your soul, any more than water is just hydrogen or just oxygen.

The Christian view is also that the body is good.[73] This doesn't mean that the body is unaffected by the fall. Due to the influence of sin, we're tempted by "bodily" sins, like lust and gluttony. But we're also tempted by "spiritual" sins, like pride and envy. But material creation is good and gives glory to God. And this is more (not less) true of the human body. When God created the rest of the physical cosmos, he called it "good" (Gen. 1:25). When he created man, body and soul, he declared his work "very good" (Gen. 1:27, 31).

These two Gnostic errors—thinking of the body as *extraneous* and as *evil*—led the Gnostics into a lot of trouble. For instance, some Gnostics denied the Incarnation.[74] After all, why would Jesus *choose* to take on flesh, if flesh is evil? Others (including Cerinthus's own followers) admitted the Incarnation, but "could not believe that a three hours' physical suffering on a cross of wood could save the world," and "bluntly denied the physical resurrection."[75] Jesus chose not to be "liberated" from his body. Instead, he rose again with that same body, glorified. To a Gnostic, that must have sounded like news that your prison cell was going to be redecorated!

In its most extreme versions, adherents of Gnosticism even argued that there were multiple gods, After all, why would a good spiritual God create evil *flesh?* And so they speculated that the evil god of the Old Testament had made the physical world and the good god of Christianity made the spiritual realm.[76]

We might reflect on the Gnostic challenge by asking three questions:

1. Am I the unity of my body and my soul, or am I just my soul?

2. Is my body a good gift from God, or is it a prison for my soul?

3. What does this mean for the body of Christ?

THE GNOSTIC CASE AGAINST THE EUCHARIST

Perhaps you're wondering why I've taken the time to outline the heresy of Gnosticism. Why drudge up ancient history? Simply put, because I don't think that the Gnostic errors are as dead as they might seem; in fact, I think they stand behind some of the arguments made against the Eucharist during the Reformation and today.[77]

For instance, John Calvin argued that "Christ, in

commending his spirit to the Father, and Stephen his to Christ, simply meant that when the soul is freed from the prison-house of the body, God becomes its perpetual keeper."[78] Notice that this is the Gnostic, not Christian, view of the body.[79] And is *exactly* the view of the body (and the human person) that the apostles fought fiercely against. Where Calvin saw the body as a "prison" for the soul, the apostle Paul said that "your body is a temple of the Holy Spirit within you," and that "you are God's temple and that God's Spirit dwells in you" (1 Cor. 3:16; 6:19). Is my body part of "me"? Paul says yes, Calvin seems to say no. And what *is* my body? Paul says a temple of God, Calvin says a prison of the soul.

Nor was Calvin alone in this Gnosticizing tendency. One of the fiercest fights *between* the early Reformers was between Martin Luther and the Swiss Reformer Ulrich Zwingli over whether to grant *any* kind of bodily presence to Christ in the Eucharist:

> If Luther's favorite text in support of his view was "This is my body," Zwingli's favorite was John 6:63, where Jesus claims "The flesh profits nothing."
>
> Coursing through the Christological debate over Christ's presence in the Supper was a strong dichotomy between flesh and spirit. For Luther, a spiritual presence with no physical local presence was not a true presence at all. For Zwingli, the belief that the bread and wine contained the physical body and blood of Christ bordered on idolatry. Zwingli continually pressed Luther on why the physical presence was necessary if the "flesh profits nothing."[80]

So there's the debate, in a nutshell. At the end of Jesus' eucharistic teaching in John 6, he says, "It is the spirit that gives life, the flesh is of no avail." Zwingli and his followers claim that this proves the Eucharist is merely symbolic. But *spirit* doesn't mean the same thing as *symbol* or *metaphor*. When St. Paul says that your body "is sown a physical body" and resurrected as "a spiritual body" (1 Cor. 15:44), we don't take him to mean that the resurrection is only a metaphor or a symbol, and not literally true. That's not a sound reading.

Neither does Zwingli's interpretation make theological or contextual sense. Foretelling both the Last Supper and Good Friday, Jesus has just finished saying that "the bread which I shall give for the life of the world is my flesh," and that "unless you eat the flesh of the Son of man and drink his blood, you have no life in you" (John 6:51, 53). To take him to be saying in v. 63 that *his* flesh is worthless wouldn't just disprove the Eucharist. It would contradict what he has just said . . . and "disprove" his death on the cross. Remember, this is exactly the Gnostic argument against Good Friday: Jesus' flesh is "of no avail," and so his bodily death does nothing.

As the Lutheran theologian Paul Althaus explains, "Zwingli and his followers were teaching the dualism and the spiritualism of late classical antiquity." (That is, Zwingli and his followers were recycling Gnosticism.) "They understood spirit as the opposite of flesh in the sense of bodiliness. For Luther, however, spirit is the opposite of flesh in the sense of sinfulness. ... Bodily eating is itself a 'spiritual' eating when it takes place in faith. For everything which is done in faith is spiritual."[81]

In other words, when Jesus speaks of the worthlessness

of "the flesh," he's not saying *his* flesh (in the Eucharist or elsewhere) is worthless. He's saying that *our* ability to understand things carnally, unaided by the Spirit, isn't going to get us anywhere. The biblical battle between "flesh" and "Spirit" isn't a battle of our bodies against our souls. Rather, it's our tendency (in both body and soul!) to resist the will of God. Paul describes "the passions of our flesh, following the desires of body *and mind*" (Eph. 2:3). Our fallen minds, as much of our fallen bodies, can be guilty of behaving "according to the flesh" (Rom. 8:13).

Paul says that "the desires of the flesh are against the Spirit, and the desires of the Spirit are against the flesh," but his list of "the works of the flesh" includes "enmity, strife, jealousy, anger, selfishness, dissension, party spirit, envy"— all of which are *spiritual* evils rather than bodily ones (Gal. 5:16-21). As St. Augustine points out, the devil (who has no body) is guilty of all of these things, so the issue "is not by having flesh, which the devil has not, but by living according to himself—that is, according to man — that man became like the devil."[82] If you're following yourself rather than God, you're living according to "the flesh," whether you're indulging in bodily pleasures (like food and sex) or spiritual pleasures (like pride).

What does this mean for John 6:63, then? Augustine explains that the flesh indeed "profiteth nothing, but only in the manner in which they understood it," since they "understood the flesh, just as when cut to pieces in a carcass, or sold in the shambles."[83] If your understanding of the Eucharist is that we kill and cannibalize Jesus, or if your understanding of Good Friday is that it's human sacrifice, then you've gravely misunderstood what Jesus is saying. You need to understand Jesus *spiritually*—not in the sense of "metaphorically" or "symbolically," but in the sense of "faithfully."

Contrast this biblical understanding to the description provided by figures like the nineteenth-century Baptist preacher Charles Spurgeon.[84] According to him, in John 6:63, "flesh is external religion, the carnal part of it, that which the eye sees and the ear hears: spirit is the inward part of religion, that which the soul understands, receives, believes, and feeds upon."[85] Jesus, in Spurgeon's view, is saying that "external religion" is "of no avail." But if "that which the eye sees and the ear hears" is of no avail, then Jesus has just called his own teaching, as well as his own death on the cross, worthless.*

Spurgeon's rejection of "external religion" is at the heart of his rejection of the Eucharist, which he calls "the greatest monstrosity of this kind in the present day." He begins his argument against the Eucharist not by carefully analyzing what the New Testament means by "flesh," but by appealing to human skepticism. In his words, the Eucharist "is monstrously absurd, I think every intelligent person knows."[86]

And from a human perspective, he has a point. Jesus' listeners raised the same objection, saying, "How can this man give us his flesh to eat?" and, "This is a hard saying; who can listen to it?" (John 6:52, 60). After Jesus refused to relent, "many of his disciples drew back and no longer went about with him" (v. 66). So, Spurgeon is right: "every intelligent person" can see how strange Jesus' teaching is. But

---

* After all, the good news proclaimed by the apostles was "that which was from the beginning, which we have heard, which we have seen with our eyes, which we have looked upon and touched with our hands, concerning the word of life" (1 John 1:1). Spurgeon's argument would seem to prove this seen, heard, and touched gospel is worthless.

as Augustine points out,[87] this appeal to human intelligence rather than divine truth is precisely what Jesus is condemning in calling "the flesh" worthless.

But to those who believe in the Eucharist, Spurgeon poses another argument:

> If Jesus Christ's body be really received into your mouth, broken with your teeth, and made to enter into your stomach, then, in the first place, you are guilty of a gross act of cannibalism and nothing better, inasmuch as you eat human flesh; and, in the next place, you cannot derive any virtue therefrom, for Jesus Christ tells you at once, "It is the spirit that quickeneth: the flesh profiteth nothing." If you did actually eat the very body of Christ, it would affect your digestive and secretive organs, and through them your flesh, just as other bread, or, if you like it better, other flesh would do; but how could this affect your heart and soul. Does grace operate through the stomach, and save us through our bowels?[88]

This is a fascinating argument, for two reasons. First, Spurgeon misunderstands the Eucharist in exactly the way that Augustine warns against, treating it as cannibalism. And second, Spurgeon seems to flatly reject the idea that grace *can* "operate through the stomach." For him, the body is apparently not a place for God's grace.

But contrast this with how he describes Adam's eating of the fruit in the Garden of Eden in Genesis 3: describing the "one act of tasting the forbidden fruit" as the one offense that "has ruined us all."[89] So Spurgeon has no problem with believing that spiritual *death* comes about by eating, but he mocks the idea that spiritual *life* can come about by eating. Sin can work through the body, but grace can't. On all of this, the Gnostics would have heartily agreed with him. So what would the early Christians say in response?

THE BIBLICAL (AND EUCHARISTIC) ANSWER TO GNOSTICISM

In imagining how the early Christians might have responded to Zwingli or Spurgeon or their modern heirs, we should remember how they responded to Cerinthus and the first generation of Gnostic thinkers.

The apostle John, for instance, denounces the Gnostics as antichrists, saying that "many deceivers have gone out into the world, men who will not acknowledge the coming of Jesus Christ in the flesh; such a one is the deceiver and the antichrist" (2 John 1:7), and Irenaeus tells us that John's Gospel was written (in part) "to remove that error which by Cerinthus had been disseminated among men."[90]

John begins his Gospel by telling us how "in the beginning was the Word, and the Word was with God, and the Word was God," that "all things were made through him, and without him was not anything made that was made" (John 1:1-2). There's one divine author of creation, spiritual *and material*. And "the Word became flesh and dwelt among us, full of grace and truth; we have beheld his glory, glory as of the only Son from the Father" (v. 14). John uses the Greek word *sarx* there: Jesus doesn't just become "man." He "became *flesh*."

In "becoming flesh," Jesus misses no opportunity to show us the falsity of Gnosticism. People bring to him "all the sick, those afflicted with various diseases and pains, demoniacs, epileptics, and paralytics" (Matt. 4:24) and Jesus heals their bodies, minds, and souls. "The blind receive their sight, the lame walk, lepers are cleansed, and the deaf hear, the dead are raised up, the poor have good news preached to them" (Luke 7:22).

And Jesus regularly communicates his divine power through material (even bodily) means. For instance, a leper approached Jesus and said, "Lord, if you will, you can make me clean." Jesus "stretched out his hand and touched him, saying, 'I will; be clean.' And immediately his leprosy was cleansed" (Matt. 8:2-3). The significance of this moment is perhaps lost on us. Leprosy was a deadly, contagious disease. For the good of the community, the Mosaic Law required lepers to keep isolated, and to warn others of their uncleanliness (Lev. 13:45-46). Anyone, even a priest, who touched a leper became ritually unclean himself (22:4-6). And yet here Jesus chooses to heal the man's leprosy by *touching* him. And rather than Jesus becoming unclean, the *leper becomes clean.*

Unlike the Gnostics, Jesus isn't put off by the grossness of the body. We might even say that he leans into it. For a blind man, Jesus "spat on the ground and made clay of the spittle and anointed the man's eyes with the clay, saying to him, 'Go, wash in the pool of Siloam' (which means Sent). So he went and washed and came back seeing" (John 9:6-7). In another case, Jesus encountered a blind man, and "spit on his eyes and laid his hands upon him" (Mark 8:23). Encountering a deaf man with a speech impediment, Jesus "put his fingers into his ears, and he spat and touched his tongue; and looking up to heaven, he sighed, and said to him, 'Ephphatha,' that is, 'Be opened'" (7:33-34). That's three separate miracles in which Jesus heals people by putting his spit on them!

I think Jesus' use of the body is summed up well by C.S.

Lewis. There's a fake Lewis quotation that says "you don't have a soul. You are a Soul. You have a body." I once fell for this, believing it was really Lewis; so did prominent Evangelicals like John Piper and Ravi Zacharias, who also shared it.[91] But the *real* C.S. Lewis strongly opposed this kind of Gnostic thinking. In *Mere Christianity*, he warns that "God never meant man to be a purely spiritual creature. That is why he uses material things like bread and wine to put the new life into us. We may think this rather crude and unspiritual. God does not: he invented eating. He likes matter. He invented it."[92] It's telling that Lewis' refutation of a Gnostic view of the human person is explicitly tied with eucharistic theology.[93]

The apostles got this connection as well. In response to the question, "Do not men receive the body and blood of Christ in the Lord's Supper?" Spurgeon argued,

> Yes, spiritual men do, in a real and spiritual sense, but not in a carnal sort—not so as to crush it with their teeth, or taste it with their palate, or digest it by the gastric juices, but they receive the Lord Jesus, as incarnate and crucified, into their spirits, as they believe in him, love him, and are comforted by thoughts of him.[94]

And if you buy into the idea that *spiritual* means *invisible* or *non-physical* or *metaphorical*, this makes sense: we "eat" spiritual food in the same way we might "chew on" an idea. But for the apostle Paul, "spiritual food" is quite literal. He refers to the manna in the desert as "spiritual food," which he then compares to the Eucharist (1 Cor. 10:3, 16-17). And the manna in the desert was *literally food*. As we read in

Exodus, "When the people of Israel saw it, they said to one another, 'What is it?' . . . Now the house of Israel called its name manna; it was like coriander seed, white, and the taste of it was like wafers made with honey" (Exod. 16:15, 31). These mysterious wafer–like substances are "spiritual food" not because they're non–physical, but because they're the physical way that God draws his people to himself.

John shows Jesus making this same connection between the manna and the Eucharist in John 6, calling himself "the living bread which came down from heaven," and saying that "if any one eats of this bread, he will live for ever; and the bread which I shall give for the life of the world is my flesh" (v. 51). It's in this context, as we've seen, that Jesus says that his "flesh is food indeed," and his blood "drink indeed," and that "he who eats my flesh and drinks my blood abides in me, and I in him" (vv. 53-56).*

After the apostles died, their disciples carried on the fight against Gnosticism. And the common response of the early Christians to Gnosticism was that *since the Eucharist is true, then Gnosticism is false.*

For instance, in about A.D. 107, we find the apostle John's disciple St. Ignatius of Antioch warning the church in Smyrna about certain heretics (seemingly the Gnostics). As Ignatius explains, "they abstain from the Eucharist and from prayer, because they confess not the Eucharist to be the flesh of our Savior Jesus Christ, which suffered for our sins, and which the Father, of his goodness, raised up again."[95] Ignatius warns that those "who speak against this gift of God,

---

* The shock and horror of Jesus' Jewish audience at such a teaching must have been rivaled by the shock and horror of the Gnostics who read John's Gospel.

incur death in the midst of their disputes," and recommends that Christians should "keep aloof from such persons, and not to speak of them either in private or in public."[96] Think about that: to the earliest Christians, if you didn't believe that the Eucharist really was Jesus' flesh and blood, you were to be *shunned as a non-Christian.*

St. Irenaeus, writing around the year 180, continues this fight along similar lines:

> Then, again, how can they [the Gnostics] say that the flesh, which is nourished with the body of the Lord and with his blood, goes to corruption, and does not partake of life? Let them, therefore, either alter their opinion, or cease from offering the things just mentioned. But our opinion is in accordance with the Eucharist, and the Eucharist in turn establishes our opinion.[97]

We'll return a bit later to this quotation and tease out *why* Irenaeus thinks the Real Presence of Christ in the Eucharist goes hand-in-glove with bodily resurrection. But for now, suffice it to say that the earliest Christians disproved Gnosticism in no small part *by pointing to the Eucharist.*

HOW THE EUCHARIST ANSWERS GNOSTICISM

Perhaps the best way to sum the theme of this chapter up is by appealing to the fourth-century Church Father, St. Gregory of Nyssa,* who said that "since the human being is

---

* We'll return to Gregory as well when we get to the bodily resurrection.

a twofold creature, compounded of soul and body, it is necessary that the saved should lay hold of the author of the new life through both their component parts."[98] As Screwtape puts it in C.S. Lewis's *Screwtape Letters*, humans are "amphibians—half spirit and half animal."[99] And Jesus came to save *us*. Not simply save our bodies or simply save our souls, but save us as the "amphibians" or "twofold creatures" that we are.

Gregory analogizes this to the antidote to a poison. Medically, we now know that "each antivenom is specific for a particular species or group of animals only."[100] But Gregory realized that basic truth even back then: the bandage has to fit the wound, and the antidote has to be the right one for that particular poison. And so, since the poison of sin has infected us in both body and soul, we need Jesus to heal us, *both body and soul*.

And what does it look like for Jesus to redeem us spiritually *and* bodily? Gregory answers that "the soul being fused into him through faith derives from that the means and occasion of salvation; for the act of union with the life implies a fellowship with the life. But the body comes into fellowship and blending with the author of our salvation in another way."[101] What's that other way? "Nothing else than that very body which has been shown to be superior to death, and has been the first-fruits of our life."[102]

So, only the body of Christ can heal us bodily. And how are we to receive him? Through eating and drinking—how else? After all, Gregory says, "in no other way can anything enter within the body but by being transfused through the vitals by eating and drinking."[103]

If the Gnostics (or John Calvin) were right, and we were

just souls trapped in bodies, then "faith alone" would be enough. By faith, our souls could find a kind of liberation from the prison of the body. But if we're instead body *and* soul, then it makes sense that Christ comes to us in both the Eucharist *and* faith. The early Christians showed that since the Eucharist was true, then Gnosticism is false. Today, we should remember the reverse, as well: since Gnosticism is false, the Eucharist can be true.

But getting this right isn't just key to appreciating the Incarnation, or understanding how Christ saves us, or seeing the dignity of our bodies, or of our self-understanding as body-soul unions. As we're about to see, the degree to which we understand the Eucharist (or conversely, the degree to which we've bought into the lie of Gnosticism) radically changes how we understand worship.

5

The Key to
TRUE WORSHIP

Jesus couldn't have been clearer on the need for worship: quoting Deuteronomy 6:13, he reminds the tempter that "you shall worship the Lord your God, and him only shall you serve" (Luke 4:8). But although most Christians are agreed on the *need* to worship God, there are huge disagreements on how to worship him properly.

In fact, there are disagreements over whether there is even such a thing as a "proper" way to worship God. But the God of the Bible certainly seems to care about how he's worshiped. In Leviticus 10, we see what happens to the sons of Aaron (the first priest) when they decide to worship God in their own preferred style: "Nadab and Abihu, the sons of Aaron, each took his censer, and put fire in it, and laid incense on it, and offered unholy fire before the Lord, such as he had not commanded them. And fire came forth from the presence of the Lord and devoured them, and they died before the Lord" (vv. 1-2). Notice, the problem here isn't that they're worshiping some other god. It's that they're worshiping the true God in an "unholy" way.

As the epistle to the Hebrews says, "even the first covenant had regulations for worship and an earthly sanctuary" (Heb. 9:1). In saying that this was true "even" in the Old Covenant, the author of Hebrews takes for granted that Christian worship also has regulations for worship.

This isn't a simple Catholic-Protestant question. Catholics often disagree with one another sharply on liturgical questions, and your experience at Mass might vary widely according to which parish you attend and what the celebrant and the congregation are like. The situation within Protestantism is even more dramatic: the Protestant liturgist James F. White traces nine different major worship traditions within Protestantism,* and there are huge variations within each of those broad traditions.

So if it's strictly inaccurate to speak of "Catholic worship" as something universal and consistent, it's wildly wrong to speak of one style of "Protestant worship." Nevertheless, we can say broadly that Catholic worship is *eucharistic.* As Pope Benedict XVI says, "In every age of the Church's history the eucharistic celebration, as the source and summit of her life and mission, shines forth in the liturgical rite in all its richness and variety" (*Sacramentum Caritatis* 3).

And it was this eucharistic worship that the Protestant Reformers identified, and decisively and intentionally broke away from. Reformers like John Calvin lamented that the devil had "blinded almost the whole world into the belief that the Mass was a sacrifice and oblation for obtaining the

---

* Lutheran, Reformed, Anabaptist, Anglican, Separatist/Puritan, Quaker, Methodist, "Frontier," and Pentecostal.

remission of sins."[104] In place of the sacrifice of the Mass, Protestants invented new manmade religious services, ultimately creating all of those different worship traditions. But as different as they are, most of them have one thing in common. As White says, "Most Protestant worship, historically and at present, has not made the eucharist its central service," and that "when the eucharist is celebrated, it is often tacked on to the end (or beginning) of the usual Sunday service."[105] So what does this rejection of the Eucharist mean for true worship?

WHEN PROTESTANT "WORSHIP" ISN'T WORSHIP

Let's start with the bad news: the problem with a good deal of Protestant worship *isn't* that it's worship done badly. It's that it's *not worship at all*. I'm not just referring to the stereotypical megachurches in which pastors preach self-help clichés under the veneer of Christianity. I'm also talking about a good deal of so-called "traditional" Protestant services. For instance, here's a prominent Baptist pastor talking about what a privilege it has been "to preach each Sunday behind one of the most, if not the most, influential, twentieth-century pulpits in the Western world," and describing the role of the pulpit in the Baptist conception of worship:

> That pulpit, like most pulpits in Baptist life, stands in the middle of the building, on center stage, so to speak. It is there to make a statement that central to Baptist worship is the preaching of the book of God to the people of God. . . . Proclamation, the preaching of the gospel, should be central to Christian

worship. The sermon is the central dynamic in the worship experience. It is the fulcrum upon which the entire service of worship hinges. Everything that comes before it should point to it, and everything that comes after it should issue out of it.[106]

That might make for a lovely religious talk, but none of what he describes there is worship. And it's an incalculable loss to go from having churches built around the altar, where Jesus Christ is truly present and is offered to the Father, to churches built around the pulpit, in which a pastor tells us what he thinks Jesus' message is.

Perhaps that sounds unfair. Some, like Biola's Barry Lietsch, would reply that Protestants are simply following the model of Jewish synagogues: "To this day Protestant worship is indebted to [synagogues'] emphasis on prayer, Scripture reading, teaching, lay involvement, and elder rule."[107]And to be sure, there are some obvious similarities between what you'd find in many a Protestant church on Sunday morning and what you would find in a first-century synagogue.

When St. Paul and St. Barnabas went into the synagogue in Pisidia, for instance, "after the reading of the law and the prophets, the rulers of the synagogue sent to them, saying, 'Brethren, if you have any word of exhortation for the people, say it'" (Acts 13:15). Paul then proceeds to preach, telling how Christ fulfills "the utterances of the prophets which are read every sabbath" (v. 27), in what appears to be a reference to the communal reading of Scripture in synagogue.

Similarly, when Jesus arrived in his hometown of Nazareth, he "went to the synagogue, as his custom was, on the sabbath day" (Luke 4:16). He stands to read, is handed the scroll of Isaiah, reads from it, and then announces that "today this scripture has been fulfilled in your hearing." (vv. 16-21). So there's readings from the Bible, followed by preaching. It looks straightforwardly like many a Protestant worship service. So what's the problem?

The problem is that Jesus didn't consider this to be worship, or even prayer. If we don't see this, it's because we tend to conflate preaching, praying, and worshiping. But to Jesus, these are three clearly distinct things. We might say that preaching is talking *about* God, praying is talking *to* God, and worship is giving God what is his due (sacrifice, divine honor, etc.). And for Jesus, these three things were done in three different places.

The synagogue is clearly a place for religious instruction and for preaching. Jesus gave the Bread of Life discourse, which we've looked at throughout this book, "in the synagogue, as he taught at Capernaum" (John 6:59). So it's a place of teaching. But it's just as clearly *not* a place of prayer.

Today, synagogues are the place where Jewish believers come together for prayer, but this wasn't the case back in Jesus' day.[108] There's a famous first-century synagogue in Jerusalem with an inscription on the floor that describes the synagogue as a place for "reading the Law and studying the commandments, and as a hostel with chambers and water installations to provide for the needs of itinerants from abroad." But as Rabbi Reuven Hammer points out, there's "no mention of prayer." He argues that "although the argument from silence is never absolute, the evidence is overwhelming that synagogues in the time prior to the destruction of the Second Temple were primarily places for the dissemination of knowledge of the Torah on a popular level, and that whatever prayer took place there was either connected to study or secondary to it."[109]

Not until the Temple in Jerusalem was destroyed in A.D. 70 did the synagogue become the primary spot for Jewish prayer. You might imagine it this way: if your local church is closed, you might gather to pray in the gym instead—perhaps, if you couldn't build or relocate to a new church, for a long time. But that doesn't mean that gyms are the primarily places that Christians gather for prayer.

If a scholar were to see you doing this and conclude that Christians must have always gathered in gyms, he'd be misreading the evidence.[110] This is what has happened with Protestant scholars who claim that "weekly synagogue worship" (a) existed at the time of Christ and (b) was *more* important to the early Christians than was Temple worship. Yet these same scholars admit that "many of our sources concerning early synagogue worship come from after the fall of the Jerusalem temple, at which point the role and practices of the synagogue shifted significantly."[111] So the obvious question they (and we) should be asking is: if the synagogue really was this all-important center of Jewish prayer during Jesus' lifetime, and for the early Christians, why is there no clear historical evidence of this from that period?

After all, it's not as if the New Testament is silent about the synagogue, or silent about prayer. Both are mentioned repeatedly. Yet we never read of anyone praying in the synagogue.[112] In fact, it's more extreme than this: the one time the synagogue *is* connected with prayer, it's Jesus saying *not to pray in the synagogue*. That's because the synagogue in Jesus' day was a place for secular business and the study of Scripture, not a place of prayer or worship. As James W. McKinnon explains,

The synagogue appears there [in the New Testament] as the proper venue for judicial and penal activities but not for prayer. Jesus warns his disciples that "they will deliver you up to councils, and flog you in their synagogues" (Matt. 10:17), and Paul recalls his pre-conversion activities: "Lord, they themselves know that in every synagogue I imprisoned and beat those who believed in thee" (Acts 22:19). As for prayer, Jesus gives this advice: "When you pray, you must not be like the hypocrites; for they love to stand and pray in the synagogues and at street corners, that they may be seen by men . . . But when you pray, go into your room and shut the door" (Matt. 6:5–6).[113]

Jesus didn't forbid praying in the synagogue because he thought synagogues were bad places. He visited them weekly, going "about all the cities and villages, teaching in their synagogues and preaching the gospel of the kingdom, and healing every disease and every infirmity" (Matt. 9:35). The synagogue is fine as a gathering spot, and it's a great place to find a crowd to whom you can preach the good news. But the implication of Jesus' words in Matthew 6 is that "the synagogue is a public place like a street corner, not a proper place for prayer."[114] The Pharisees and hypocrites weren't praying in the synagogue because it was a house of prayer (it wasn't); they were praying there because it was a public place (like a street corner) where they could be seen acting piously.

So where *should* we pray? Anywhere and everywhere, as long as we're not ostentatious about it.

Paul says to "pray constantly" (1 Thess. 5:16), and we find several places (again, with the notable exception of the synagogue) in which Jesus and his followers pray: in one's room (Matt. 6:6), in "a lonely place" (Mark 1:35), in the Garden of Gethsemane (Matt. 26:36), in the Upper Room (Acts 1:14), and most importantly, in the Temple. While cleansing the Temple, Jesus points out that it's described in the Old Testament as "a house of prayer" for all the nations (Isa. 56:7; Mark 11:17). This continued to be true of the early Christians: Peter, John, and Paul are each mentioned as going into the Temple to pray (Acts 3:1; 22:17).

Although *prayer* could take place in the Temple, it didn't have to. (And the goal of the Christian life is to learn how to pray always, wherever you are.) In contrast, worship *did* have to be in the Temple. Contrary to the numerous Protestant scholars who claim that there was something called "synagogue worship" at the time of Jesus, the Samaritan woman says explicitly, "Our fathers worshiped on this mountain [Mount Gerizim]; and you say that in Jerusalem is the place where men ought to worship" (John 4:20). So, unlike prayer, worship *had* to be in the Temple.

That means, of course, that the Jews of Jesus' day (including, apparently, Jesus himself) understood there to be an important difference between prayer and worship. Certainly they are connected: Luke says that the prophetess Anna "did not depart from the temple, worshiping with fasting and prayer night and day" (Luke 2:37). But they're also distinct. So what do Jesus and the Samaritan woman mean by "worship"? As Protestant scholar Everett Ferguson explains, "Sacrifice was the universal language of worship in the ancient world."[115] Although they could *pray* anywhere, the Samaritans could only offer ritual *sacrifices* on Mount Gerizim (where, in fact, they continue to do so),[116] and Jews could only offer ritual *sacrifices* in Jerusalem.

Take careful note that Jesus doesn't say that he's abolishing worship, since no more sacrifice will be necessary after Calvary. Instead, he calls for a *new way* of sacrificing, "when the true worshipers will worship the Father in spirit and truth, for such the Father seeks to worship him" (John 4:23). We'll unpack the deeper meaning of *that* provocative claim in a moment, but for now, notice that Jesus is saying that Christian worship is still sacrificial worship, just in a new form.

This is indispensable for rightly understanding Christian worship. There's nothing wrong with gathering together to read Scripture and discuss its meaning or to listen to an expert tell you what it means. That can be an important help in your spiritual journey; it was for Jesus, who was in the custom of attending synagogue weekly (Luke 4:16). But this can't fill our spiritual need for prayer, and still less for worship. So if we're serious about worshiping in a biblical way, what does that look like?

TRUE WORSHIP: PAST, PRESENT, AND FUTURE

Part of the answer to that question is to step back and look at the big picture . . . by which I mean the *really* big picture: the whole cosmic story of worship laid out in the Bible, a story that connects past, present, and future.

Let's start with the past. In the Old Testament, what did true worship look like? Well, we could say that it was *sacrificial*, *ritual*, *communal*, and *multisensory*.

As Fr. Robert Daly put it, "The sacrificial ritual was the

center of the religious life of ancient Israel."[117] These sacrifices were ordered toward divine communion. Paul says as much, comparing them to the Eucharist: "Consider the practice of Israel; are not those who eat the sacrifices partners in the altar?" (1 Cor. 10:18). And we see this throughout the Old Testament as well. Remember how Moses offered "the blood of the covenant" and then (along with Aaron, Nadab, Abihu, and seventy of the elders of Israel) "saw the God of Israel," and, beholding God, "ate and drank" (Exod. 24:8-11).

And this sacrificial ritual of communal worship involved sacred sights, sacred sounds, sacred smells, sacred tastes, and sacred touches. For instance, God had the priestly vestments adorned with "a golden bell and a pomegranate" (Exod. 28:33-34) so that you could recognize the priest not only by his look but by the sound of his walk! There was a special blend of incense whose scent could *only* be used in worship (Exod. 30:22-33); there were particular sacrifices to be eaten by particular people for particular causes (Lev. 7).

Eventually, all of this comes to take place in the Temple, where the architecture further reinforces the beauty of the ritual. The Jewish Talmud quotes the ancient sages as saying, "One who has not seen Herod's building has never seen a beautiful building in his life."[118] But "Herod's building," the Second Temple, was nothing compared to the prior glorious Temple that God instructed King Solomon to build. God says as much: "Who is left among you that saw this house in its former glory? How do you see it now? Is it not in your sight as nothing?" (Hag. 2:3).

If Catholics can seem, at times, unduly interested in the liturgy and architecture, we're only following God's lead. And indeed, the similarities between the Mass and Israel's liturgy has been one of the criticisms regularly made against Catholicism. The Reformed theologian Loraine Boettner described the Mass as "a recrudescence* of Judaism," saying that "its ceremonialism stands much closer to Judaism than to New Testament Christianity." He claims that this reveals a fascination "with the beauty of the temple and its gorgeous ritual."[119] But the Bible is clear that ritual *should* be gorgeous.

The Mass is also intentionally bodily and multisensory. The whole body is involved, with set times for kneeling, standing, sitting, and processing up toward the altar. The beauty of the church should draw the eyes toward God, while the beauty of the music does the same for the ears and the incense does the same for the nose, and so on. And in the Eucharist, even taste and touch are drawn into the worship of God.

Both the past Temple and the present Mass are pointing toward something that (for those of us on earth) still lies in the future: the heavenly liturgy. When God gave Moses the instructions for the first tabernacle, he said, "According to all that I show you concerning the pattern of the tabernacle, and of all its furniture, so you shall make it" (Exod. 25:9). The epistle of the Hebrews points to this moment as proof that the Old Testament system serves "a copy and shadow of the heavenly sanctuary" (Heb. 8:5). That's significant, because it means that heavenly worship is like the worship of the Old Testament, only better.

What does that heavenly worship look like? It's described at length in the book of Revelation†—and the liturgy that

---

* Recrudescence: the recurrence of something undesirable.

† This is significant, since many Christians claim that the New Testament is silent on what worship looks like.

John describes doesn't look like what you might find in a Protestant megachurch or neighborhood Bible chapel. It looks much more like the Temple liturgy and the Mass: there are harps and "golden bowls full of incense, which are the prayers of the saints" (Rev. 5:8-9), with worship centered around the throne, inside "God's temple in heaven," with "the ark of his covenant" within it (11:19). It's multi-sensory worship centered around the real presence of God.

After this, John sees "a new heaven and a new earth; for the first heaven and the first earth had passed away" (Rev. 21:1). And in the new Jerusalem, John says, "I saw no temple in the city, for its temple is the Lord God the Almighty and the Lamb" (v. 22). In Revelation, this perfect and eternal communion between God and man is described as "the marriage supper of the Lamb" (19:9).

The bride to whom the Lamb is married is, of course, the Church.

Paul says that Genesis 2:24 (which says that "a man shall leave his father and mother and be joined to his wife, and the two shall become one flesh") is "a great mystery, and I mean in reference to Christ and the church" (Eph. 5:31-32). For Paul, marriage points toward this ultimate communion between Christ and the Church; John sees that union's fulfillment, describing "the holy city, new Jerusalem, coming down out of heaven from God, prepared as a bride adorned for her husband; and I heard a great voice from the throne saying, 'Behold, the dwelling of God is with men. He will dwell with them, and they shall be his people, and God himself will be with them'" (Rev. 21:2-3).

And so just as true Christian worship should remind us of the worship of Jerusalem of old, it should also prepare us for the worship of the New Jerusalem. In the words of the

Second Vatican Council, "In the earthly liturgy we take part in a foretaste of that heavenly liturgy which is celebrated in the holy city of Jerusalem toward which we journey as pilgrims, where Christ is sitting at the right hand of God, a minister of the holies and of the true tabernacle" (*Sacrosanctum Concilium* 8). Or as Pope Benedict XVI puts it:

> With its vision of the cosmic liturgy, in the midst of which stands the Lamb who was sacrificed, the Apocalypse [the book of Revelation] has presented the essential contents of the eucharistic sacrament in an impressive form that sets a standard for every local liturgy. From the point of view of the Apocalypse, the essential matter of all eucharistic liturgy is its participation in the heavenly liturgy; it is from thence that it necessarily derives its unity, its catholicity, and its universality.[120]

A good gauge of how well we're worshiping, then, is how similar our worship is to what St. John saw.*

WORSHIPING GOD IN SPIRIT AND TRUTH

Most forms of Protestant worship *don't* look like what you'd find in either the Temple or the New Jerusalem—and by

---

* By the way, this also explains why Catholic homilies tend to be a lot shorter than Protestant sermons. Pope Francis notes that although a good preacher "may be able to hold the attention of his listeners for a whole hour," the risk is that "his words become more important than the celebration of faith." Instead, the context of the eucharistic liturgy means that "the words of the preacher must be measured, so that the Lord, more than his minister, will be the center of attention" (*Evangelii Gaudium* 138).

design. As Evangelical theologian Robert Webber explains, the Reformation brought about a "shift from the visual to the spoken word" in worship. No longer was truth to be "mysteriously acted out in the liturgy." Instead, "truth was in the Bible and the Bible alone."[121]

Webber says that this shift "can be seen in the structure of Protestant worship, which focuses on the reading and preaching of Scripture; in the architecture, which is plain; and in the hymns, which reinforce and teach the message of the Bible."[122] Couple that with the Reformers' rejection of the sacrifice of the Mass,[123] and you're left with liturgies that don't look like what an ancient Israelite or early Christian would have recognized as divine worship.

There are various theological defenses for this shift. One of them, which we've already seen, is the idea that Christian worship is supposed to look like the synagogue rather than the Temple.[124] But I want to consider here two other (somewhat related) arguments: (1) the idea that Christ abolished these ritual ways of worship in the tearing of the Temple veil, and (2) the idea that Christian worship should be simplified so that it's done "in spirit and truth."

Regarding the first argument, here's how one Protestant author characterizes the relationship between the prayer of Israel and the prayer of the Church:

> When one of the disciples asked Jesus to teach them how to pray, Jesus replied: "When you pray, say: Our Father in heaven, hallowed be your name" (Luke 11:1). For his disciples, the thought of ordinary people being able to pray directly to God would have been unusual—hence the question. Following the tearing of the temple veil, enabling access for all

who wish to draw near to God, the sacrifice of himself, a type of veil (Heb. 10:20), is the (only) way that
we can approach God.[125]

I've heard variations of this claim from numerous Protestants over the years: that (1) the Israelites didn't (or even
couldn't) pray directly to God, which is why they had to go
to the priest instead; (2) but then Jesus abolished the priesthood (and indeed, *any* earthly priesthood), enabling us to
go directly to God, and (3) the tearing of the Temple veil
symbolizes Jesus' rejection of intermediaries.

But nearly every part of this claim is false. And what's the
core problem? Once again, it's confusing *prayer* and *worship*.
Ordinary Israelites *did* pray directly to God, regularly, and
they didn't have to be in the Temple to do so.* Jesus' disciples aren't asking him *if* they can pray, they're asking him
how they ought to pray, since John the Baptist had given his
disciples a model for prayer (Luke 11:1).

And Jesus isn't abolishing intercessory prayer, either, as
his apostles attest. Paul is explicit "that supplications, prayers,
intercessions, and thanksgivings be made for all men" (1
Tim. 2:1), just as he is explicit in asking others to pray for
him (Eph. 6:18-19; 2 Thess. 3:1-2). And St. James tells us to
"confess your sins to one another, and pray for one another,
that you may be healed" (James 5:16).

So, Jesus doesn't seem to be abolishing priests or

---

* For instance, the Israelites in slavery in Egypt (Exod. 2:23; Deut. 26:7),
or Manoah (Samson's father) praying for guidance for what to do with their
son (Judg. 13:8), or Hannah praying in the Temple for a child (1 Sam. 1:10),
or Tobit and Sarah (Tob. 3:1, 11), etc. When Job's friend Eliphaz thought
Job had sinned against God, he said "you will make your prayer to him,
and he will hear you" (Job 22:27).

intercessory prayer, or creating a novel concept that believers can pray directly to God. What, then, *is* the significance of the tearing of the temple veil? Hebrews 9 and 10 answer that question in two ways.

First, Jesus offers the perfect sacrifice. We no longer need to slay animals, since we can plead the blood Christ offered once for all on the cross (Heb. 9:26). We looked at this angle in more detail back in chapter two: remember the difference—and connection—between Preparation Day and the Passover meal. Second, Jesus gives us a new place of worship: a new Temple, and a new Holy of Holies (Heb. 10:19*ff*).

This is also the answer to the other objection. I promised earlier that we'd get back to Jesus' famous response to the Samaritan woman, that "God is spirit, and those who worship him must worship in spirit and truth" (John 4:23-24). As the Presbyterian scholar Ronald Byars explains, "Among Protestants, it's been common to quote John 4:23 as though Scripture proves that the best way of worship doesn't use physical things or engage the body at all."* But he asks, "Where did we get the idea that 'spirit' and the material world are in opposition to one another? That sort of dualism owes more to Greek thought, or Zoroastrianism or the Manichean heresy than it owes to biblical faith."[126] In other

---

* The Protestant theologian Robert Webber says that the Reformation brought about a "shift from the visual to the spoken word" in worship. No longer was truth "mysteriously acted out in the liturgy." Instead, "truth was in the Bible and the Bible alone." Webber says that this shift "can be seen in the structure of Protestant worship, which focuses on the reading and preaching of the Word; in the architecture, which is plain; and in the hymns, which reinforce and teach the message of the Bible" (*Ancient-Future Faith: Rethinking Evangelicalism for a Postmodern World* (Grand Rapids: Baker books, 1999), p. 98).

words, it's that same Gnostic misunderstanding of "spirit" as "non-physical" that we looked at in the last chapter.

So, what's the right way to understand this?

Jesus is promising that in the New Covenant, sacrificial worship will continue. But it'll be radically different in form and no longer tied to a single location (like Mount Gerizim or the Temple in Jerusalem). This is the fulfillment of one of the Old Testament promises made through the prophet Malachi. Rebuking the priests of Israel by telling them "I have no pleasure in you" and "I will not accept an offering from your hand," God foretells that there will come a day in which true worship will be offered by "the nations" (that is, the Gentiles): "for from the rising of the sun to its setting my name is great among the nations, and in every place incense is offered to my name, and a pure offering; for my name is great among the nations" (Mal. 1:11).

Jesus is telling the Samaritan woman that this time has now come. The sacrificial offerings can now be offered any-where on earth, from the rising to the setting of the sun.* How can this be? Because the Christian Temple is *Jesus' body*: wherever the Holy Spirit makes the Son present, this worship may be offered to the Father.[127] If you understand

---

* This connection between the Malachi prophecy and the Mass is made in Eucharistic Prayer III, which declares that "you never cease to gather a people to yourself, so that, from the rising of the sun to its setting, a pure sacrifice may be offered to your name." The early Christians regularly made this connection, as well. For instance, around the year 150, St. Justin Martyr points to the Malachi prophecy to show how "God, anticipating all the sacrifices which we offer through this name, and which Jesus the Christ enjoined us to offer, i.e., in the Eucharist of the bread and the cup, and which are presented by Christians in all places throughout the world, bears witness that they are well-pleasing to him" (*Dialogue with Trypho* 117, ANF 1:257–58).

this shift—that our temple is now the Body of Christ—you'll understand the truly radical shift that occurs from the animal sacrifices of the Old Testament to the sacrifice of the Mass.

THE CHRISTIAN TEMPLE

Although it's tempting to think that Christ abolishes the role of the Temple in worship, that's not quite right. Rather, he offers us a *new* Temple: his body. John says this explicitly in his Gospel, in a passage too-often overlooked. When Jesus says, "Destroy this temple, and in three days I will raise it up," John explains that "he spoke of the temple of his body" (John 2:19, 21). What would it mean to take this idea seriously?

The last eight chapters of Ezekiel are all about the coming of a new and miraculous temple. Among the many prophecies about it, one is that streams of miraculous living water would flow from its side (Ezek. 47:1-12).* But there are good reasons to believe that this wasn't about a literal building. Instead, this prophecy is fulfilled on Good Friday. There on the cross, "one of the soldiers pierced his side with a spear, and at once there came out blood and water" (John 19:34). So there's life-giving blood and water flowing from the side of Christ.

---

* Another is that it would be surrounded by a Temple gate facing east, and that "this gate shall remain shut; it shall not be opened, and no one shall enter by it; for the Lord, the God of Israel, has entered by it; therefore it shall remain shut" (Ezek. 44:2). The early Christians saw in this a prophecy of Mary's perpetual virginity: since God himself enters the world through her womb, she doesn't go on to bear other children. Whether you agree with this reading or not, it's a good indication that the early Christians understood Ezekiel to be prophesying Christ, not a literal building.

The early Christians saw several layers of meaning here. In one layer, this was recognized as a sign of the life-giving role of baptism and the Eucharist. As St. John Chrysostom (347-407) wrote, "It is from both of these that the Church is sprung through the bath of regeneration and renewal by the Holy Spirit, through baptism and the mysteries."[128] In another, the early Christians also saw in this a sign of something else: the creation of Eve (Adam's bride) from his side.[129] As the *Catechism* puts it, "As Eve was formed from the sleeping Adam's side, so the Church was born from the pierced heart of Christ hanging dead on the cross" (CCC 766).

If Christ is the "last Adam" (1 Cor. 15:45), and the Church is his bride (Eph. 5:25-33), this makes sense: he forms the Church from his life-giving blood and water. The rib from the side of Adam forms his bride Eve, the streams of water from the side of the prophesied Temple are lifegiving, and the blood and water flowing from the side of Christ are life-giving (in baptism and the Eucharist) and are the means by which Jesus creates his bride, the Church.

But there's still another layer of meaning here. In the Temple of Jerusalem, there were actually two sets of temple veils. The Jewish priests could go beyond the first one to perform their ritual duties, but even they couldn't go beyond the second temple veil. The only one who could do that was the high priest, and he could only do it once a year, on Yom Kippur, when he offered the atoning sacrifice (Heb. 9:6-7).

On the other side of that second temple veil was the Holy of Holies, the holiest place in the world. In the Holy of Holies (at least originally) was the Ark of the Covenant, where God promised to meet with his people (Exod. 25:22).

And per Hebrews 9:4, there were three other signs of God's presence there: the manna, the "bread from heaven" (Exod. 16:4); the staff of the first high priest Aaron, since the priest "stands to minister there before the Lord your God" (Deut. 17:12); and the Ten Commandments, "the two tables of the testimony, tables of stone, written with the finger of God" (Exod. 31:18). Calling Christ the new Temple, therefore, invokes the idea of both *atoning sacrifice* and *divine presence*.

Hebrews 10:19-20 thus says that "we have confidence to enter the sanctuary by the blood of Jesus, by the new and living way which he opened for us through the curtain, that is, through his flesh" (Heb. 10:19-20). In other words, the piercing of the side of Christ *is* the tearing of the true Temple veil (that's the "curtain" he's talking about). The "new and living way" we experience the divine presence is through the "blood and water." Through baptism and the Eucharist, we experience directly (not through any intermediary) the true Holy of Holies.

But amazingly, there's even more to this. When Eve is formed from the side of the sleeping Adam, he sees in her an extension of himself, "bone of my bones, and flesh of my flesh," and it's here that we're told that "therefore a man leaves his father and his mother and cleaves to his wife, and they become one flesh" (Gen. 2:23-24). In other words, Eve "completes" Adam, and is "one flesh" with him. As I mentioned above, Paul saw this as a prophecy of Christ's "one flesh" union with the Church (Eph. 5:31-32), and he sees the Church as Christ's "body, the fulness of him who fills all in all" (1:23). As the body of Christ, this means that the Church is also "a holy temple in the Lord" (Eph. 2:19-21).

This is true in the big sense of the whole Church, but there's also a sense in which, since each of us is part of the body of Christ, and the body of Christ is a Temple, *each of our bodies is a temple.* Jesus applies the Ezekiel 47 prophecy about the water flowing from the side of the Temple to *us,* saying, "He who believes in me, as the scripture has said, 'Out of his heart shall flow rivers of living water,'" to which John adds, "this he said about the Spirit, which those who believed in him were to receive" (John 7:38-39).

And that's exactly where Paul takes this idea: "Do you not know that your body is a temple of the Holy Spirit within you, which you have from God?" (1 Cor. 6:19). In other words, the shocking new Christian message isn't that we can now "pray to God directly." The shocking new Christian message is that our God wants to dwell in *us,* in our bodies, as he once dwelt in the Temple in Jerusalem.

And so, Paul continues, "glorify God in your body" (1 Cor. 6:20). Elsewhere, he writes, "I appeal to you therefore, brethren, by the mercies of God, to present your bodies as a living sacrifice, holy and acceptable to God, which is your spiritual worship" (Rom. 12:1). Whereas many Protestants have (mis)understood "worship in spirit and truth" to mean something disembodied, for Paul it means the exact opposite. Spiritual worship *is* bodily worship.

So, the Christian concept of the new Temple is threefold: Christ's body (on the cross and in the Eucharist), the Church, and our own bodies.

First, it's sacrificial worship centered around the Temple of Christ's body. Second, it's the sacrificial worship of the body of Christ. And third, it's sacrificial worship we offer in the temples of our own bodies. As St. Augustine says, "A true sacrifice is every work which is done that we may be united to God in holy fellowship, and which has a reference to that supreme good and end in which alone we can be truly blessed."[130]

In other words, when you offer up the daily sufferings of your life, or make sacrifices for God and neighbor, or "offer up a sacrifice of praise to God" (Heb. 13:15),* you're acting as the priest in the temple of your body. And you do this as part of the "holy temple in the Lord" known as the Church. As Pope Benedict XVI says, "The new worship appears as a total self-offering made in communion with the whole Church" (*Sacramentum Caritatis* 70).

At Mass, this threefold sense of "temple" aligns perfectly. We offer our meager self-offerings to be united to Christ's perfect self-offering. In Augustine's words, "this is the sacrifice of Christians: we, being many, are one body in Christ. And this also is the sacrifice which the Church continually celebrates in the sacrament of the altar, known to the faithful, in which she teaches that she herself is offered in the offering she makes to God."[131]

---

* This explains how we can describe the moral life as spiritual worship (CCC 2031) or talk about the need to "continually offer up a sacrifice of praise to God, that is, the fruit of lips that acknowledge his name" (Heb. 13:15).

6

The Key to
RESURRECTION

The Second Vatican Council says that when we receive the Eucharist, "Christ is eaten, the mind is filled with grace, and a pledge of future glory is given to us."[132] But what does "a pledge of future glory" mean?

It turns out, this idea goes back to the beginnings of Christianity. Earlier, I promised to return to an argument that St. Irenaeus made back around the year 180. In his battle against the Gnostics, he asked, "How can they say that the flesh, which is nourished with the body of the Lord and with his blood, goes to corruption, and does not partake of life?"[133]

This passage is famous for what he says next ("Our opinion is in accordance with the Eucharist, and the Eucharist in turn establishes our opinion"), but that's not the part I want to focus on here. Instead, I want to highlight how Irenaeus takes it for granted that there's some link between the Eucharist and bodily resurrection. That's sounds like an odd claim to our ears, doesn't it? Yet we find it all over the place in the writings of the earliest Christians.

For instance, back around the year 107, the apostle John's disciple St. Ignatius of Antioch described the Eucharist as "the medicine of immortality, and the antidote to prevent us from dying, but [which causes] that we should live forever in Jesus Christ."[134] He warned that those "who speak against this gift of God, incur death in the midst of their disputes. But it were better for them to treat it with respect, that they also might rise again."[135] Ignatius doesn't just say that rejecting the Eucharist is damnable, although he's clear about that. He also says that the Eucharist and eucharistic reverence are key to our bodily resurrection on the last day. So where does this strange idea come from?

From Jesus.

The first person to connect the ideas of the Eucharist and bodily resurrection was the Lord, when he said that "he who eats my flesh and drinks my blood has eternal life, and I will raise him up at the last day" (John 6:54). The early Christians didn't invent the idea of a connection between the Eucharist and bodily resurrection; it's something that they—and Jesus—seem to take for granted. But we might still ask: just what *is* this connection?

Fortunately, some of the early Christians answer that question. I want to focus on the answer given by one of them in particular: the fourth-century bishop and theologian St. Gregory of Nyssa, a major figure in the early Church.[136] His argument goes into some depth, but I will highlight its four major steps.

In context, Gregory is actually answering a somewhat different question: "How can that one body of Christ vivify the whole of mankind, all, that is, in whomsoever there is faith, and yet, though divided among all, be itself not diminished?"[137] In other words, when I receive the Eucharist, does that mean that there's now a little bit less of Jesus' body? And Gregory is going to answer that by saying *no*, there's actually a little *more* of Jesus' body, because I'm now more fully incorporated in it. But his journey in showing this also helps make sense of the connection between the Eucharist and resurrection.

STEP ONE

Jesus Turns Bread and Wine Into
His Body and Blood . . . Naturally!

Here's a question for Protestant readers (or to ask your Protestant friends): *Do we see any moments in the Bible where Jesus turns bread and wine into his body and blood?* Now, depending on your views of the Eucharist, you might say no. But look at Luke 7:34, in which Jesus says, "The Son of man has come eating and drinking; and you say, 'Behold, a glutton and a drunkard, a friend of tax collectors and sinners!'"

As Gregory put is, when Jesus "came in a body such as ours," he "did not innovate on man's physical constitution," but instead "secured continuance for his own body by the customary and proper means."[138] We could imagine a world in which Jesus created a body for himself that had no need of food or drink; it was certainly *possible*. But instead, he took to himself a human body that hungered and thirsted (see Luke 4:2) like anybody else's. And what did Jews of Jesus' day eat? They "partook of a typical Roman-Mediterranean cuisine—the triad comprised of bread, wine, and olive oil," and we have evidence of ancient rabbinical blessings for both bread and wine.[139]

So although this might seem like a funny way of putting

it, there's no question that Jesus turned bread and wine into his body and blood. He did it countless times, in the same way we turn food and drink into our bodies and blood every day: through metabolism. Once we realize this, we're ready to consider the miracle of the institution of the Eucharist.

STEP TWO

Jesus Turns Bread and Wine Into
His Body and Blood . . . Supernaturally!

At the Last Supper, Jesus again changes bread and wine into his body and blood. Only this time, Gregory says, it's *not* "by the process of eating to the stage of passing into the body of the Word." Instead "it is at once changed into the body by means of the Word."[140]

Gregory is hardly the only early Christian to be fascinated by this connection between the Incarnation and the institution of the Eucharist. In the Incarnation, "the Word became flesh" through his own divine power (John 1:14). That is, Jesus' virgin-born body is itself a miracle. In the institution of the Eucharist, the Word makes flesh through the word.* St. Ambrose (the famous bishop of Milan who helped to convert St. Augustine) once explained the Eucharist to a group of catechumens about to be baptized, and then said,

> Perhaps you will say, *I see something else, how is it that you assert that I receive the body of Christ?* And this is the point which remains for us to prove. And what

---

* That is, Jesus works this miracle *through speaking*, just as God once spoke the cosmos into existence.

evidence shall we make use of? Let us prove that this is not what nature made, but what the blessing consecrated, and the power of blessing is greater than that of nature, because by blessing nature itself is changed.[141]

Ambrose is arguing that the word of God is so powerful that it can transform nature. He gives a number of Old Testament examples from Moses and Elijah to show "that grace has more power than nature," even when we're speaking only of "the grace of a prophet's blessing."[142] But then he comes to the point:

But why make use of arguments? Let us use the examples he gives, and by the example of the Incarnation prove the truth of the mystery. Did the course of nature proceed as usual when the Lord Jesus was born of Mary? If we look to the usual course, a woman ordinarily conceives after connection with a man. And this body which we make is that which was born of the virgin. Why do you seek the order of nature in the body of Christ, seeing that the Lord Jesus himself was born of a virgin, not according to nature? It is the true flesh of Christ which crucified and buried, this is then truly the sacrament of his body.[143]

In other words, why would we expect the body of Christ, *which itself exists only because of the supernatural Incarnation,* to be bound by nature? Hasn't Jesus already shown himself superior to nature?

I love Ambrose's argument by itself. But I also like to

pair it with Gregory's argument. Where Ambrose focuses on Christ's supernatural *superiority* to nature, Gregory focuses on the resemblance between what the Father institutes naturally and what Christ institutes supernaturally.

C.S. Lewis, in his book *Miracles*, looks at the miracles that Jesus performs and puts them each into one of six groups: miracles of fertility, of healing, of destruction, of "dominion over the inorganic," of reversal, and of "perfecting or glorification."[144] Looking at all of Jesus' miracles, Lewis notices something remarkable: that in each miracle, Jesus "does suddenly and locally something that God has done or will do in general. Each miracle writes for us in small letters something that God has already written, or will write, in letters almost too large to be noticed, across the whole canvas of Nature."[145]

For instance, Jesus turns water into wine at the wedding feast of Cana (John 2:1-12). But you know what else turns water into wine? Grapes. They just do it slowly and naturally, whereas Christ does it instantaneously and supernaturally. Jesus multiplies fish; but leave the fish alone long enough, and they'll multiply themselves. Jesus heals the sick; but so does your body. The point here isn't to belittle Jesus' miracles in any way, but rather to point out how everything Jesus does supernaturally resembles something that God is already doing in the order of nature.

Contrast this organic quality of miracles with fairy tales (where pumpkins turn into stagecoaches) or the devil's temptations (to turn stones into bread). There's nothing in nature like a pumpkin that becomes a stagecoach, or like a stone that turns into bread. Those false miracles are "arbitrary and meaningless violations of the laws of Nature."[146] The devil's idea of a miracle mocks nature; Jesus' miracles glorify nature. That's because Jesus loves the order of nature:

after all, "all things were made through him, and without him was not anything made that was made" (John 1:3). So although Jesus goes *beyond* nature, he never goes *against* it.*

Lewis calls this the "hereditary style"—that is, the "family style."[147] Gregory is showing us that the Eucharist has all the hallmarks of it. What Jesus ordinarily did slowly and naturally (step one), he now does instantaneously and supernaturally (step two). This miracle has divine fingerprints all over it. But Gregory's explanation doesn't stop there.

STEP THREE

Jesus "Metabolizes" Us Into His Body

What's the effect of receiving the Eucharist? Gregory describes the Eucharist as our bodily "fellowship and blending with the author of our salvation."[148] In his words, Jesus "disseminates himself in every believer through that flesh," "blending himself with the bodies of believers." [149] It's this "fellowship and blending," this union with Christ, that we should explore here. According to Gregory, the eucharistic elements are not only changed into the body and blood of Jesus; the Eucharist changes *our* bodies from mortal flesh to

---

* Even the central mysteries of Christianity—Christ's incarnation and resurrection—have a certain parallel with the natural world. In Lewis's words, "In the Christian story God descends to reascend. He comes down; down from the heights of absolute being into time and space, down into humanity; [...] but he goes down to come up again and bring the whole ruined world up with him." But Lewis argues that we see this pattern written "all over the world" in the procreation of plants and animals. For instance, a plant "must belittle itself into something hard, small, and deathlike, it must fall into the ground: thence the new life reascends" (*Miracles*, p. 180). Jesus is the first to draw this parallel, saying that "unless a grain of wheat falls into the earth and dies, it remains alone; but if it dies, it bears much fruit" (John 12:24).

"union with the immortal."[150] In the Eucharist, we receive Jesus. But there's another sense in which *he* receives *us*, "metabolizing" us (as it were) into his body. In the words of then-Cardinal Joseph Ratzinger,

> It is truly the one, identical Lord, whom we receive in the Eucharist, or better, the Lord who receives us and assumes us into himself. St. Augustine expressed this in a short passage which he perceived as a sort of vision: 'Eat the bread of the strong; you will not transform me into yourself, but I will transform you into me.'[151]
>
> In other words, when we consume bodily nourishment, it is assimilated by the body, becoming itself a part of ourselves. But this bread is of another type. It is greater and higher than we are. It is not we who assimilate it, but it assimilates us to itself, so that we become in a certain way "conformed to Christ," as Paul says, members of his body, one in him.[152]

We can understand this in two ways. The first way is that we are *collectively* metabolized into the body of Christ. Our initiation into Christ begins at our baptism (Gal. 3:27). But this is completed—consummated—in our eucharistic communion.* The body of Christ in the Eucharist forms the body of Christ, the Church. This is exactly what Paul says to the Corinthians: "Because there is one bread, we who are many are one body, for we all partake of the one bread" (1 Cor. 10:17). We don't merely celebrate the Eucharist because

---

* For this reason, first communion has historically been the last of the three "sacraments of initiation" (baptism, confirmation, Eucharist) a new Christian receives.

we're one. In a real way, we are one *because* we celebrate a common Eucharist. Or as Paul says, "Now you are the body of Christ and individually members of it" (1 Cor. 12:27).

This is important to remember because, as strange as it might sound, we Catholics sometimes forget that communion is communal. It's possible to fall into a mindset in which we go to Mass to receive grace, and Jesus, and our neighbors in the pews are just a distraction. Maybe you wonder, "Why is it important to go to Mass on *Sunday*? Why can't I just go throughout the week, when it's quieter?" But the truth is, a purely "personal" relationship with Jesus, cut off from our relationship with our neighbors, isn't Christian.

Love of God and love of neighbor are inseparable (see Matt. 22:36-40). In the words of the apostle John, "If any one says, 'I love God,' and hates his brother, he is a liar; for he who does not love his brother whom he has seen, cannot love God whom he has not seen" (1 John 4:20). It's for this reason that we come together for *corporate* worship. The epistle to the Hebrews reminds us to "consider how to stir up one another to love and good works, not neglecting to meet together, as is the habit of some, but encouraging one another, and all the more as you see the Day drawing near" (Heb. 10:24-25).

Addressing a group of newly baptized Christians on the verge of receiving their first Communion, Augustine said, "Receive and eat the body of Christ, yes, you that have become members of Christ in the body of Christ; receive and drink the blood of Christ. In order not to be scattered and separated, eat what binds you together; in order not to seem cheap in your own estimation, drink the price that was paid for you."[153]

So that's the first sense in which, through the Eucharist,

Jesus metabolizes us into his body: by incorporating us more deeply into his Church and by binding the Church together. And this is also why those who are out of full communion with the Church are not ordinarily invited to receive the Eucharist: because it's a communion with Christ the head *and* his body the Church.[154]

As Benedict XVI says, "Communion always and inseparably has both a vertical and a horizontal sense: it is communion with God and communion with our brothers and sisters. Both dimensions mysteriously converge in the gift of the Eucharist" (*Sacramentum Caritatis* 76). This means that Christian unity can never come about by our mere human efforts, but must be the fruit of our union with God—a union that God effects in many ways, but none greater than in the Eucharist.*

But there's another sense in which we can understand being metabolized into the body of Christ: a *spiritual transformation* occurs within us. This transformation is called many things—divinization, deification, glorification, *theosis*—and the first time you hear about it, you might be tempted to cry heresy!

The idea is simple. Jesus didn't come into the world

---

* Specifically, our union with God enables us to love our neighbor, and it's through this love of God and neighbor that the Church is made one. But this also means that every sin (through which we damage our communion with God) harms our relationship with the Church. As Pope St. John Paul II explains, "There is no sin, not even the most intimate and secret one, the most strictly individual one, that exclusively concerns the person committing it. With greater or lesser violence, with greater or lesser harm, every sin has repercussions on the entire ecclesial body and the whole human family" (*Reconciliatio et Paenitentia* 16). Or in the words of St. Paul, if one member of the Body of Christ suffers, "all suffer together; if one member is honored, all rejoice together" (1 Cor. 12:26).

merely to be with us. He didn't come merely to save us from our sins or merely to rise from the dead or merely to bring us to heaven. All of those things happened, and are good, and are part of God's plan, but God's plan is greater. Christ the Word became "what we are, that he might bring us to be even what he is himself."[155] He doesn't just want us to be *with* him. He wants us to be *like* him. Or in the shocking words of St. Athanasius (c. 296–373), God "was made man that we might be made God."[156]

Before we get to what this idea means (and what it doesn't!), it's worth asking: is this idea biblical? The New Testament actually contains various references to divinization. John writes, "Beloved, we are God's children now; it does not yet appear what we shall be, but we know that when he appears we shall be like him, for we shall see him as he is" (1 John 3:2). So we *already* possess divine sonship. What's coming next is somehow beyond this, and something we haven't seen yet, but we know that it involves being made *like Christ*.

Paul says something similar: that "we all, with unveiled face, beholding the glory of the Lord, are being changed into his likeness from one degree of glory to another; for this comes from the Lord who is the Spirit" (2 Cor. 3:18). He calls us "children of God, and if children, then heirs, heirs of God and fellow heirs with Christ, provided we suffer with him in order that we may also be glorified with him" (Rom. 8:16–17). But these present sufferings are nothing compared to the glory to come, since "this slight momentary affliction is preparing for us an eternal weight of glory beyond all comparison, because we look not to the things that are seen but to the things that are unseen" (2 Cor. 4:17–18). So, then, we are to receive an "eternal weight of glory beyond all comparison," becoming "heirs of God" and being changed into Christ's own likeness.

Paul's connection between sonship and divinization is important. One of the theological controversies in the first century revolved around the Roman emperor, Caesar Augustus, being called *divi filius*, "son of god."[157] The Jews and early Christians rightly recognized this as blasphemy. When Jesus of Nazareth came into the world, presenting himself as the true Son of God, his Jewish listeners were no less outraged. John says that they "sought all the more to kill him" because he "called God his Father, making himself equal with God" (John 5:18). Today we use the phrase "child of God" so casually that we tend to forget this, but in calling yourself a "child of God," you're making a *divine claim*.

Jesus' listeners try to stone him for this blasphemy (John 10:33). But Jesus responds in a strange way. Quoting Psalm 82:6, he asks, "Is it not written in your law, 'I said, you are gods'? If he called them gods to whom the word of God came (and Scripture cannot be broken), do you say of him whom the Father consecrated and sent into the world, 'You are blaspheming,' because I said, 'I am the Son of God'?" (vv. 34-36). So Jesus agrees: being a child of God *is* a divine claim, but it's one that *God himself makes for the children who receive his word.*

The final New Testament source to consider is Peter, who talks about the divine power that "has granted to us all things that pertain to life and godliness, through the knowledge of him who called us to his own glory and excellence" (2 Pet. 1:3).[158] We are called to glory; in fact, to God's own glory. Peter connects this with God's "precious and very great promises"—that through them, we may "become partakers of the divine nature" (v. 4). There's divinization, laid bare: Christ came into the world to partake of our human nature, so that we could become partakers of the divine nature.

The early Christians were (quite rightly) fascinated by this idea. St. Irenaeus even warned against those who would deny it, and thereby "defraud human nature of promotion into God."[159] What makes this more fascinating is that the Christians are proclaiming this idea of divinization while rejecting the Roman imperial version, in which the emperor becomes a god after his death. (This started after the death of Julius Caesar, which is why his adopted son Augustus called himself "son of God"). And St. Justin Martyr, writing in response to this idea around the year 160, said that Christians "have learned that those only are deified who have lived near to God in holiness and virtue; and we believe that those who live wickedly and do not repent are punished in everlasting fire."[160] In other words, the Romans were *right* to believe in deification, but wrong about who is deified, or how it occurs.

As the Christian doctrine of deification is different from the Roman imperial version, it's also different from the Mormon idea of "exaltation." Joseph Smith, the founder of Mormonism, denied that God the Father is the uncreated Creator of everything, claiming instead that God is a man from another planet who became "exalted." In his words, God the Father "dwelt on an earth, the same as Jesus Christ himself did," and that he "was once as we are now, and is an exalted man."[161]

In turn, Mormons claim that we (or at least they) will eventually become gods of our own planets. Spencer Kimball (the twelfth LDS president) taught that "each one of you has it within the realm of his possibility to develop a kingdom over which you will preside as its king and god. You will need to develop yourself and grow in ability and power and worthiness, to govern such a world with all of its people."[162] This is what Lorenzo Snow (the fifth LDS president) called a "continual course of progression": we become gods of our own planets, and create people who then become gods of their own planets, and so forth.[163] Leaving aside the logical and theological problems with such a scheme (does God's god have a god? Is there an infinite regress of "gods," or is there one god over all creation?), let's be clear that this *isn't* the Christian teaching.

So what *is* the Christian teaching? Athanasius clarifies that when we speak of becoming "children of God" or even "gods," we mean "not as he in nature and truth, but according to the grace of him that calleth."[164] God, who is all-knowing, shines his light on us to see what we otherwise couldn't. God, who is all-powerful, equips us to do things that would be impossible for mere men. And God, who is all-loving, enables us to love one another with his own divine love. When Jesus says, "Be merciful, even as your Father is merciful" (Luke 6:36), he's calling us to live in a divine way. And he calls us to share even in God's omnipotence, saying of salvation, "With men it is impossible, but not with God; for all things are possible with God," and that "all things are possible to him who believes" (Mark 9:23, 10:27).

You can think of the difference between the Mormon and the Christian views by envisioning divine life like electricity, and God as the power plant. The Mormon view is that we can become "exalted" to become power plants ourselves. The Christian view is that we're like light bulbs. Without the power from the plant, we can do nothing. But if we're open to it—if our switch is on and we're connected to the power plant—the power will flow through us. If we allow ourselves to be totally transformed by God's grace, then we can someday say with St. Paul, "I have been crucified with Christ; it is no longer I who live, but Christ who lives in me; and the life I now live in the flesh I live by faith in the Son of God, who loved me and gave himself for me" (Gal. 2:20).

But here's where the lightbulb analogy reaches its limits. God isn't just lighting up what's already in us by nature. Through his grace, God is continually expanding and transforming us, taking us from dim bulbs to something unbelievably luminous; a transformation fueled by "the immeasurable greatness of his power in us who believe" (Eph. 1:19).

As C.S. Lewis put it, we "live in a society of possible gods and goddesses" in which "the dullest and most uninteresting person you talk to may one day be a creature which, if you saw it now, you would be strongly tempted to worship, or else a horror and a corruption such as you now meet, if at all, only in a nightmare."[165] That's the Christian vision of divinization. But as luminous and godlike as the saints in glory are, they're not rivals to God. After all, God is the source of all that is good within them, now and forever. And so God is "glorified in his saints" (2 Thess. 1:10), not threatened by them.

So what does this radical promise of divinization have to do with Christ's gift of his body and blood in the Eucharist? The Christian version of divinization is all about our union with "incorruptibility and immortality,"[166] and we experience precisely this union in receiving the Eucharist.

In the words of St. Cyril of Jerusalem (A.D. 313-386), "By partaking of the body and blood of Christ, may [we] be made of the same body and the same blood with him.

For thus we come to bear Christ in us, because his body and blood are distributed through our members; thus it is that, according to the blessed Peter, 'we become partakers of the divine nature.'"[167] So through the Eucharist we are divinized, because we partake of the divine nature.

In response to those who thought that Jesus was just "some man" who *became* God, Athanasius responds that "we are deified not by partaking of the body of some man, but by receiving the Body of the Word himself."[168] It's a remarkable passage: he simply takes for granted that the Eucharist deifies us, and then uses this to prove that Jesus is more than a mere human.

STEP FOUR

By "Metabolizing" Us,
Jesus Preserves Us from Corruption

And with that, we have arrived at the final step: what does any of this have to do with the resurrection?

Gregory says that Jesus "infused himself into perishable humanity" so that "by this communion with Deity mankind might at the same time be deified."[169] To that end, Christ "disseminates himself in every believer through that flesh, whose substance comes from bread and wine, blending himself with the bodies of believers, to secure that, by this union with the immortal, man, too, may be a sharer in incorruption."[170] But why does being metabolized into Christ mean that we share in incorruption?

Here, it's helpful to cast our minds back to an age before preservatives and refrigeration. In those days, the lifespan of bread and wine was fleeting. "Daily bread" literally meant just that—any longer than a day and it went moldy. And wine had a small window before it turned sour.

So how do you avoid moldy bread and wine that tastes like vinegar? By *eating the bread and drinking the wine.* They won't go bad inside us. Although this may sound like a strange way to put it, we preserve the bread and wine from corruption by eating and drinking them.

Our bodies "preserve" bread and wine through eating and drinking because what had previously been bread and wine is now incorporated into our body. Yet our bodies are themselves destined for corruption. Without some remedy, we'll rot forever. If you spend your life worshiping your own flesh, you'll find that once you're "planted" in the grave, your god can only decompose and fall apart. Somehow, instead, "this perishable nature must put on the imperishable, and this mortal nature must put on immortality" (1 Cor. 15:53).

Fortunately, we have a remedy in the flesh of Christ. As Scripture says, Christ "was not abandoned to Hades, nor did his flesh see corruption" (Acts 2:31). God "raised him from the dead, no more to return to corruption" (Acts 13:34). Just as we preserve bread and wine from corruption by metabolizing them into our bodies, Christ preserves us from corruption by metabolizing us into his incorruptible body.

Irenaeus says that this is like how "a grain of wheat falling into the earth and becoming decomposed, rises with manifold increase by the Spirit of God, who contains all things, and then, through the wisdom of God, serves for the use of men, and having received the word of God, becomes the Eucharist, which is the body and blood of Christ."[171] He's alluding to Jesus' words in John 12:24 that "unless a grain of wheat falls into the earth and dies, it remains alone; but if it dies, it bears much fruit" (John 12:24). And Irenaeus's point is that, in the Eucharist, the grain of wheat dies, bears much fruit . . . and then is miraculously transformed into Christ.

But Christ doesn't just want to transform grain into his divine body. He wants to transform *us* into his divine body.* Irenaeus says that "our bodies, being nourished by [the Eucharist], and deposited in the earth, and suffering decomposition there, shall rise at their appointed time, the word of God granting them resurrection to the glory of God, even the Father, who freely gives to this mortal immortality, and to this corruptible incorruption."[172]

It's a fascinating promise. Yes, we'll die, and yes, our mortal bodies will rot in the grave for a time. But if we're nourished by the Eucharist, metabolized into the incorruptible flesh of Christ, we know that someday we we'll rise again with immortal, incorrupt, glorified resurrection bodies. Or to put it another way, "He who eats my flesh and drinks my blood has eternal life, and I will raise him up at the last day" (John 6:54).

---

* It's worth remembering that Irenaeus isn't some late medieval theologian, whom we might accuse of overthinking things or of being biased by centuries of Catholic traditions. Irenaeus was a student of St. Polycarp, who was himself a disciple of the apostle John. He is writing in about A.D. 180, a year before the first recorded use of "Trinity," and it's from this same Irenaeus that we first learn that Christians use the Gospels of Matthew, Mark, Luke, and John.

7

The Key to the
SAINTS

On February 4, 1912, a tailor in Paris by the name of Franz Reichelt climbed 187 feet up the Eiffel Tower, wearing "a voluminous black overcoat" with "pounds and pounds of heavy fabric," and a "strange, high-framed hood."[173] His mission: to prove to the world that he had invented the world's first functional parachute jacket, one seemingly modeled off of the biology (or at least the appearance) of a bird.[174]

Reichelt had fooled the powers-that-be into letting him up there by telling them he was just going to test his new invention by strapping a dummy into it and throwing it off of the tower.[175] But he had no such intention. He explained his plan by saying that "I want to try the experiment myself and without trickery, as I intend to prove the worth of my invention."[176] And so try it he did, jumping (or falling) out of the Eiffel Tower . . . and dropping immediately to the ground. He died instantly.

It's a tragic story. But it's also a good reminder that

sometimes, ideas that make sense in our heads don't work in real life. And maybe you're asking a similar question right now about all of this Eucharist stuff. *Does it work in real life?*

Answering that question is the aim of these last two chapters, in which we'll look at the eucharistic spirituality of the saints and at our own spiritual life.

Why start with the saints? Partially because of something Pope Benedict XVI said. In an interview he gave long before becoming pope, he described what he saw as the "only really effective apologia"—that is, defense—for Christianity. If you know Benedict's reputation as a brilliant thinker, maybe you're expecting some complicated theological argument. But he doesn't say anything like that. Instead, he said, "The only really effective apologia for Christianity comes down to two arguments, namely the *saints* the Church has produced and the *art* which has grown in her womb."[177]

The point here isn't that sound theology and reasoned explanations for the Faith are unimportant. Benedict knew better than to claim that. But he also knew that when you're going through a dark time—whether it's a personal tragedy, or a crisis of faith, a scandal in the Church, or some other kind of struggle—you probably don't want (or need) an intellectual argument, even a true one. (That's the mistake that Job's friends made in the book of Job.) Instead, you need to see God's goodness, beauty, and love *in action*. And one of the greatest and most undeniable ways that we see those things is in the lives of the saints.

This is also, in fact, perfectly sound theologically. At the Last Supper, Jesus says, "I am the vine, you are the branches. He who abides in me, and I in him, he it is that bears much fruit, for apart from me you can do nothing" (John 15:5). At a minimum, this means that there are certain things in life (whether it's some good work, or incredible endurance in the face of adversity, etc.) that are *only* attainable through divine grace.

In response to those who denied his teachings, Jesus says, "If I am not doing the works of my Father, then do not believe me; but if I do them, even though you do not believe me, believe the works, that you may know and understand that the Father is in me and I am in the Father" (John 10:37-38). Jesus can't both be teaching falsehood *and* performing divine works; his works validate his teachings. And he says to his followers that "he who believes in me will also do the works that I do; and greater works than these will he do" (14:12). So we should see in the saints the kind of lives that we couldn't lead without God's assistance.

In this chapter, then, I want to put the spotlight on four of the countless saints whose lives were animated by the Eucharist.* My interest is particularly in those people who performed seemingly impossible feats and credited these feats to their faith in the Eucharist. Having placed their trust in Jesus Christ in the Eucharist, they—unlike poor Franz Reichelt—*soared*.

ST. SATYRUS OF MILAN AND EUCHARISTIC CONVERSION

Satyrus (c. 331-c. 378) was on a journey from Italy to Africa when he was shipwrecked off the coast of the island of Sardinia. At the time, Satyrus was not yet "initiated in the

---

* Entire books could be (and have been) written just on the theme of this chapter. As Benedict remarks, "Holiness has always found its center in the sacrament of the Eucharist" (*Sacramentum Caritatis* 94).

more perfect mysteries," meaning (at the least) that he hadn't received confirmation and the Eucharist, and possibly that he was still unbaptized.* And so, as the ship was foundering in rocky shoals, Satyrus was afraid: not of shipwreck or of dying, but of the idea that "he should depart this life without the mystery," going to the grave without ever partaking of the Eucharist.[178]

This led him to do something remarkable: he "asked of those whom he knew to be initiated the divine sacrament of the faithful; not that he might gaze on secret things with curious eyes, but to obtain aid for his faith."[179] He knew that, even in these extreme circumstances, he wasn't to receive the Eucharist, particularly if he was still unbaptized. He had a different plan. Somehow, he convinced whoever it was who had the Blessed Sacrament aboard (perhaps a priest, but the text doesn't say) to put it in a scarf or cloth, which was then tied around Satyrus's neck.

And then, he "cast himself into the sea, not seeking a plank loosened from the framework of the ship," but trusting that he would be saved by this eucharistic faith alone. It was a wild plan: instead of doing the ordinary thing of grabbing onto something that floats, he simply kept the Eucharist close to him. And, remarkably, *it worked*: Satyrus "was sufficiently protected and defended by this."[180]

Once ashore, Satyrus "offered thanks and brought away faith":

---

* In a footnote to the text, an editor (presumably Philip Schaff) explains that "many holy men postponed baptism, not out of contempt or carelessness, but through fear, in all the dangers of the period, of losing baptismal grace, sin after baptism and grace received being then estimated at its true awfulness."

> For he who had felt such protection on the part of the heavenly mystery wrapped in a napkin, how much did he expect if he received it with his mouth and drew it to the very depth of his bosom? How much more must he have been expecting of that, when received into his breast, which had so benefited him when covered with a napkin?[181]

He also knew what he had to do next. It was time to come home to the Catholic Church. And so he approached a bishop and—aware of the danger of schism—"enquired whether he agreed with the Catholic bishops, that is, with the Roman Church?" Once he was sure the bishop was Catholic, he was received into the Church without delay.[182]

Perhaps in reading this story, you're skeptical, thinking it sounds too much like a "Golden Legend"—one of those stories of the saints that gets bigger and bigger over the years until it no longer bears any resemblance to the truth. I can appreciate that skepticism, but I don't think it's necessary here. All of the details I've just shared come from the homily preached at St. Satyrus's funeral a few years later by his famous younger brother, St. Ambrose. This isn't some medieval legend; it is a nearly contemporaneous account of what happened, told by the brother of the man to whom it happened. And not just any brother, but a reputable one: the bishop of Milan, a man St. Augustine described in his *Confessions* as a bishop "known to the whole world as among the best of men."

I include this Satyrus as the first of the four saints, both because I think it's a remarkable story, and because I think Satyrus stands for all the innumerable converts for whom the Eucharist was a magnet that drew them in the midst of their doubts and questions.

ST. FRANCIS XAVIER AND EUCHARISTIC EVANGELIZATION

If Satyrus is a reminder that Christ draws us toward himself in the Eucharist, other saints remind us that Christ also strengthens in the Eucharist to go out toward others. Take St. Francis Xavier (1506-1552), for instance, one of the greatest missionaries of all time. Historians believe that Francis *personally* converted and baptized something like 30,000 people throughout his missionary journeys.[183] What makes his success as a missionary particularly striking is that he didn't have any of the modern mass media tools (or means of transportation) that we possess today.

Instead, he personally traveled across southern and eastern Asia, traveling by ship, and preaching the Gospel "in season and out of season" (2 Tim. 4:2). Francis preached both to those who had never heard of Christianity and to those who had grown cold in their faith. His missions took him to what are now the nations of India, Sri Lanka, Malaysia, Indonesia, and Japan.[184] His ultimate hope was to preach to the Chinese, but he died on the Chinese island of Shangchuan without ever reaching the mainland.

What fueled Francis's missionary zeal? In no small part, his love of the Eucharist. The people of Goa, India, where Francis had set up what we might call his base of operations, had a number of stories about him. One told about how Francis would spend a "great part of his days and nights in prayer, which he usually made in a *coretto* or small 'tribune' adjoining the church, from which he could see the altar of the Blessed Sacrament," and where he would be found transfixed in prayer, his eyes "inflamed with tears" and his face "all aglow."[185]

The people of Goa also claimed that "out of devotion to the Blessed Sacrament" he was known "to administer Holy Communion upon his knees instead of standing, and once he was seen to float in this attitude along the rail to give the sacred particles to the people."[186] Whether you regard these stories as strict history or pious exaggerations, they certainly speak to how the people of Goa understood Francis: as a man of prayer, deeply in love with Jesus Christ in the Eucharist.

It was this love that enabled him to succeed in missionary journeys that were fraught with dangers and hardships. In one of his letters, Francis writes to a fellow Jesuit to warn him of the trials that new missionaries can expect to face:

> To give some idea of the difficulties which those destined for Japan will encounter when they appear in the universities: they will be continually assailed with questions and disputes one after another, they will be the sport of the people, mocked and laughed at by everyone.
>
> In fact, so many importunate people come at every instant that barely a moment can be found for bodily needs, for taking a little sleep or food. Satan will lay snares for them in wonderful ways, and our brethren deprived of their hours of divine meditation and office, and above all of the fruits of the most Holy Eucharist, if they have added to this the persecution of the *bonzes* [Buddhist monks], the excessive inconvenience of the cold, the insufficiency

and difficulty about food, and the absolute hopeless absence of all human consolation and aid—these, I say, who have to undergo so many and such great miseries, must be endowed with singular virtue.[187]

But of all the hardships he faced, Francis said that "the most grievous trial of all" while he was in Japan was that "the long distances do not allow of our carrying the articles necessary for the Holy Sacrifice, and so one has to suffer the privation of that heavenly Food, which 'strengthens the heart of man,'* and which is the only consolation for every trouble. This is the greatest misery we have in these parts."[188]

ST. MAXIMILIAN KOLBE AND EUCHARISTIC HEROISM

Nearly 400 years later, another missionary arrived in Japan: this one, a young Franciscan friar named Fr. Maximilian Kolbe (1894-1941). Within a month of his arrival in Nagasaki (a city with a Catholic population tracing back to Francis Xavier), Fr. Kolbe and two other Franciscans, despite having no money, no prior contacts in the country, and no knowledge of the Japanese language,[189] had managed to start the first Catholic magazine in Japan, *Seibo no Kishi*, distributing thousands of copies.[190]

Perhaps this seems like a small thing. But to those who saw it, it wasn't. One Japanese witness, testifying at Kolbe's canonization process (in which the Catholic Church

---

* Francis is applying to the Eucharist the words of Psalm 104:15, in which the Psalmist praises God for "wine to gladden the heart of man, oil to make his face shine, and bread to strengthen man's heart."

investigates whether he lived the life of a saint), said that "it is hardly possible to imagine how the magazine *Seibo no Kishi* could have been published by purely human means, without any knowledge of the language, without the necessary premises, and without money."[191] And this was simply the first month. By the time he left the country six years later, its circulation had risen to 65,000.[192] Throughout it all, as a later biographer would say, it was "thanks to the Eucharist alone" that Fr. Kolbe "was able to persevere in Japan and produce much fruit by his missionary activity."[193]

But it's not for his missionary activities in Japan that we primarily remember Maximilian Kolbe. Back in his native Poland, he had established a monastery called Niepokalanów, meaning the "City of the Immaculate." And "city" was an apt description: within twelve years of its founding, it had become the largest monastery in the world.[194] Once again, the growth seemed superhuman. As Pope St. John Paul II would later observe,

> To those visiting the "City of the Immaculate" who were amazed at the works accomplished, St Maximilian Kolbe, pointing to the Blessed Sacrament, explained: "The whole reality of Niepokalanów depends on this." He addressed the eucharistic Jesus with words of deep faith: "Your Blood flows in my blood; your soul, O God incarnate, penetrates my soul, strengthening and nourishing it." This was the secret of his holiness. The graces which sustain missionaries in their daily work of evangelization radiate from the Eucharist.[195]

In another time and place, perhaps this is where Kolbe's story would have ended: as a man plagued by serious (at times, seemingly life-threatening) illnesses who nevertheless shone as a missionary and as the founder of a religious community. But history intervened further. The Germans invaded Poland, and in short order, Kolbe was one of the thousands of Catholic priests imprisoned in Poland by the Nazi occupiers. Before long, Kolbe was taken to the notorious death camp of Auschwitz.

In fact, Auschwitz was worse than a death camp; it was a place where the guards actively attempted to strip prisoners of their human dignity, to shame and humiliate them, and to desecrate what they held sacred. One of Kolbe's biographers describes how "German soldiers took photographs to send to their families and there is a picture of a prisoner decorated as Christ, wearing a wreath of thorns with soldiers taunting him, 'Let Christ help you now — the SS rule here.'"[196]

Such was the atmosphere in which Kolbe spent the final months of his life, enduring special abuse on account of being a Catholic priest.[197] Although he could clandestinely hear the confessions of other prisoners, it was nearly impossible to offer Mass, due to the difficulty in getting bread and (especially) wine and to risk of getting caught.* Nevertheless, we know of two instances in which Fr. Kolbe risked his life to offer Mass for a group of thirty of his fellow prisoners.[198]

In the face of these conditions, Kolbe showed supernatural strength. Tadeusz Pietrzykowski, a fellow prisoner who

---

* His mother Marianna, who knew that he had been sent to Auschwitz, would later recall, "I suffered most when he could not attend Holy Mass or take communion." What a striking insight into the vibrant eucharistic faith of both mother and son!

was a member of the Polish Resistance, described the "almost crazy courage" of the priest, saying:

> Everybody was starving and a man is an egoist when he's starving and doesn't care what is going on; all he can think about is getting a bit of bread. It was not only the last sacrifice of Maximilian Kolbe which was remarkable but his whole behavior in the camp. He often offered himself to be beaten in place of someone else and he always shared his rations.[199]

That leads us, then, to that last sacrifice, the most famous moment in St. Maximilian Kolbe's life. It all began toward the end of July 1941, when the Nazis discovered that one of their prisoners had escaped the camp. As revenge, the infamous *Lagerführer* (camp leader) Karl Fritzsch and the SS officer Gerhard Palitzsch selected ten men at random to suffer a particularly cruel death: stripped naked and placed in cells without food and water until they perished.

Fr. Kolbe wasn't one of the ten men chosen, but a Polish army sergeant by the name of Franciszek Gajowniczek was. When he was chosen, Gajowniczek cried out, "My poor wife and children!" Such a reaction was not unexpected. What *was* unexpected was what happened next:

> Suddenly a slight figure stepped out of line, took off his cap and moved with halting gait to stand at attention before the SS. He had a flushed face, sunken eyes and cheeks and wore round glasses in wire frames. Prisoners craned to see, because although forlorn cries were not uncommon, no one had ever dared to break rank. It was probably because it was

something incomprehensible that Kolbe was not shot where he stood. Fritzsch, who had never before had conversation with a prisoner, asked: "What does this Polish pig want? Who are you?" Kolbe replied, "I am a Catholic priest. I want to die for that man; I am old; he has a wife and children."[200]

Amazingly, it worked.

It's worth stressing here that the men to whom Kolbe was speaking were awful even by Nazi standards. Fritzsch was the first to use Zyklon B to murder prisoners by the hundreds in gas chambers[201] and Palitzsch was described by his own boss, the Auschwitz commandant Rudolf Höss, as "so emotionally hardened that he could kill incessantly without sparing a single thought on his actions," and "the only one of the men who were immediately involved in the exterminations who did not once approach me in a quiet moment and unburden his heart on the horrific procedure."[202]

So why in the world did they say yes to the exchange? Perhaps the request was so shocking that it caught them momentarily off guard, or perhaps Kolbe's explanation appealed to Nazi prejudices against the weak and elderly. But still . . . why not simply kill the "Polish pig" along with Gajowniczek? Whatever it was that motivated Fritzsch and Palitzsch in this moment, it's clear what motived Fr. Kolbe: a supernatural strength that not one of us can muster apart from divine grace.

That, certainly, seems to be the biblical view. In addition to the various New Testament texts about need for divine grace, St. Paul says, "While we were yet helpless, at the right time Christ died for the ungodly. Why, one will hardly die for a righteous man—though perhaps for a good man one will dare even to die. But God shows his love for us in that while we were yet sinners Christ died for us" (Rom. 5:6-8). People don't just agree to be killed—to be stripped and slowly starved to death—for complete strangers. That's divine love in action.

The early Christians often described martyrdom in sacrificial and eucharistic terms. For instance, Paul tells the Philippians that he's ready "to be poured as a libation upon the sacrificial offering of your faith" (Phil. 2:17), and St. Ignatius of Antioch prepares for his martyrdom by telling the Christians of Rome, "I am the wheat of God, and let me be ground by the teeth of the wild beasts, that I may be found the pure bread of Christ."[203] The connection makes sense: Christ's sacrificial death is the model for all Christian martyrdom, and eucharistic grace gives the martyrs their resolve. As Ignatius goes on to say,

> My love has been crucified, and there is no fire in me desiring to be fed; but there is within me a water that lives and speaks, saying to me inwardly, "Come to the Father." I have no delight in corruptible food, nor in the pleasures of this life. I desire the bread of God, the heavenly bread, the bread of life, which is the flesh of Jesus Christ, the Son of God, who became afterward of the seed of David and Abraham; and I desire the drink of God, namely his blood, which is incorruptible love and eternal life.[204]

Similarly, we can say that "thanks to the Eucharist alone," Maximilian Kolbe lived a life of continuous self-sacrifice for others, becoming obedient unto death, even death in a starvation cell (cf. Phil. 2:8).

ST. TERESA OF CALCUTTA
AND EUCHARISTIC ENDURANCE

In 1999, the polling firm Gallup twice asked Americans who they considered the most admirable person of the twentieth century. The first time, the question was open-ended: respondents could answer with anyone they thought of. The second time, respondents chose from a list of eighteen popular candidates. But in both cases, the result was the same: in something of a landslide, people chose Mother Teresa (1910–1997).[205]

Although there are no similar worldwide polls, it's safe to say that Americans were hardly alone in their esteem for her. When she died in 1997, some 13,000 people (including ten Catholic cardinals, several heads of state, and visitors from numerous countries) attended Mother Teresa's funeral, while millions more watched it on television around the world.[206] More importantly, she left behind the Missionaries of Charity, which by the time of her death already had 4,000 sisters operating in 123 different countries.[207]

Of course, popularity and idolization (figurative or literal)[208] are no proof of holiness, and plenty of men and women try to help the poor. What made Mother Teresa so special? Pope Benedict XVI suggests,

> The answer to those who ask why Mother Teresa became so famous is simple: because she lived in a humble and hidden way, for love and in the love of God. She herself said that her greatest reward was to love Jesus and to serve him in the poor. Her slight figure, her hands joined, or while she was caressing a sick person, a leper, someone dying, or a child, is

the visible sign of a life transformed by God. In the night of human sorrow she made the light of divine love shine out and helped so many hearts to rediscover that peace which God alone can give.[209]

Let's flesh that "simple" answer out a bit, because there are two features that I think are worth mentioning about this saint.

The first is the way in which she seemed to effortlessly combine loving Jesus and serving him in the poor. Perhaps this only seems remarkable if you've ever tried to do both. Too often, we end up in one of two places instead. Either we slide into a complacent Christianity, in which we say all the right things about God but have little contact with the poor and needy—in which "the poor and needy" are a nameless, faceless group—or we can practice social justice in a way that loses sight of Christ, filling hungry bellies but not hungry souls.

But St. Teresa of Calcutta possessed a rare ability to see Christ in the poor, and to serve him in the poor. And it's what made her ministry stand out both from so many other Christian ministries, but also from so many other secular charities. In her words, "our work is not social work, it's religious work."[210]

But the second feature, oft remarked upon, was the relentlessness (one might even say fanaticism) of her love for "the least of these." It's what John Paul II would later call her "single-minded and unstinting dedication to the Lord's call."[211] Where the rest of us would have quit, she kept going. And this was the theme of her whole life. Born to a financially comfortable family in the city of Skopje, in one of the poorest corners of Europe, Anjezë Gonxhe Bojaxhiu knew from an early age she was called by God to serve him in India.[212] She did this first as a teaching sister for the Sisters of Loreto and then as the foundress of her own religious order, the Missionaries of Charity, whose purpose was "to quench the infinite thirst of Jesus Christ on the cross for love of souls" by "laboring at the salvation and sanctification of the poorest of the poor."[213]

The nature of this work and its squalid conditions was often stomach-turning, and also (both then and now) frequently unappreciated or even resented. For instance, in 1952 when she opened a free hospice (*Nirmal Hriday*) in an abandoned temple to Kali, the Hindu goddess of destruction, some Hindus were so outraged that a mob formed, with people throwing rocks and bricks at the ambulance bringing the dying to the hospice. Eventually, locals demanded that the police evict the foreigner. But when the police chief entered the hospice, he found Mother Teresa tending the purulent sores of a man who had been picked up off the street. Satisfied, the police chief returned outside and told the crowd, "I promised you that I would expel this foreign woman. And I will do so on the day that you persuade your mothers and sisters to come here and do what she is doing."[214]

And this is a sufficient answer to most of Mother Teresa's critics: starting with no money or medical expertise, she did an enormous amount of good, due to her tireless advocacy for the poorest of the poor in Calcutta. Which of her critics can say the same?

Mary Poplin, one of the numerous non-Catholics who were drawn to Mother Teresa, spent two months with her in Calcutta. She was later asked: "Non-Christians also do social justice. What made Mother Teresa's work special, and could one do her work without following Jesus?" She replied,

> That's a great question because it's the first question people really have in their minds. Well, I was only there two months and the thing that Mother Teresa had, I believe, that was different is she had God actually working through her. Through prayer, they stayed very peaceful and very satisfied with what they were doing. I think, for most of us, that work would've been so monotonous; after a while we wouldn't have had the perseverance. We've had a lot of projects at the graduate university and service-learning projects for students, but what we find is after the initial enthusiasm wears off, there's nothing there to keep them going.[215]

Poplin wasn't alone in noticing this. In 2014, a group of researchers studying Christian mental health professionals in high-stress environments observed how "spirituality provides a basis for an enhanced quality of life as individuals embrace a set of transcendental ideals that give purpose and meaning to their career pursuits," and was shown to reduce "compassion fatigue" and increase "compassion satisfaction."[216] Fittingly, they dubbed this phenomenon the "Mother Teresa Effect."

Where an ordinary person might burn out after two weeks, Mother Teresa had something—or rather, Someone—who kept her going in the worst of conditions, from the founding of the Missionaries of Charity in 1950 until her death in 1997. Fortunately, someone *did* ask her where her strength came from—her biographer Navin Chawla (a Hindu). He replied,

> The Mass is the spiritual food that sustains me. I could not pass a single day or hour in my life without it. In the Eucharist, I see Christ in the appearance of bread. In the slums, I see Christ in the distressing disguise of the poor—in the broken bodies, in the children, in the dying. That is why this work becomes possible.[217]

This is the recipe, from the lips of a saint. What made it possible for Mother Teresa to see Christ in the poor was first seeing him in the Blessed Sacrament. What gave her the strength to endure decades of caring for the poorest of the poor was the Eucharist.

Making this even more remarkable is that when she said this, she was in the midst of a terrible spiritual trial, of the sort that would make her physical trials pale by comparison. In a 1957 letter to Fr. Joseph Neuner, a priest she knew and respected, Mother Teresa revealed how since 1949 or 1950 (shortly after beginning what would become the Missionaries of Charity), she had felt "this terrible sense of loss—this untold darkness—this loneliness—this continual longing for God." In her words:

> Sometimes I just hear my own heart cry out "My God" and nothing else comes. The torture and pain I can't explain. From my childhood I have had a most tender love for Jesus in the Blessed Sacrament—but this too has gone. I feel nothing before Jesus—and

yet I would not miss Holy Com. [Communion] for anything.[218]

Fortunately, Fr. Neuner recognized that this spiritual darkness wasn't the result of anything Mother Teresa was doing wrong, but was "the special share she had in Jesus' passion." That is, Jesus was inviting her to join him in the darkest moments of Good Friday, when human suffering seemed most pointless, when God seemed most absent. But her darkness was also, as Fr. Brian Kolodiejchuk put it, "an identification with those she served: she was drawn mystically into the deep pain they experienced as a result of feeling unwanted and rejected and, above all, by living without God."[219] Realizing that God desired her to experience this darkness, she embraced it, and went to him there . . . staying with him in that darkness for much of the nearly half-century she lived.

✳✳✳

As I was writing this chapter, I realized that—quite unintentionally—I had chosen four saints whose relationship with the Eucharist was . . . complicated. St. Satyrus loved Jesus in the Eucharist, but couldn't receive it because he wasn't Catholic yet. St. Francis Xavier and St. Maximilian Kolbe loved Jesus in the Eucharist but couldn't receive more often, because it was logistically impossible. And St. Teresa of Calcutta, Mother Teresa, loved Jesus in the Eucharist but didn't come away from her time with him feeling emotionally buoyed or spiritually filled (even as she *was* being spiritually filled).

The way Jesus worked so visibly and miraculously in each

of their lives should be heartening for all of us who find our own relationship with him complicated for any whatever reason. If you show up and give him your all, even if your all is weak and imperfect, he'll more than do the rest. But how *can* we give him a little more? That's the last question for us to consider.

8

The Key to Your
SPIRITUAL LIFE

If Mother Teresa was the easy choice for most-admired person of the twentieth century, C.S. Lewis's *Mere Christianity* was the easy choice for the most-influential Christian book.[220] Like Mother Teresa, Lewis was to undergo a spiritual trial—sparked by the death of his wife, Joy. One of the insights that this trial offered him was "only a real risk tests the reality of a belief."[221] For it's very easy for us to say we believe in Jesus until we have to actually act upon that belief. In Lewis's words,

> You never know how much you really believe anything until its truth or falsehood becomes a matter of life and death to you. It is easy to say you believe a rope to be strong and sound as long as you are merely using it to cord a box. But suppose you had to hang by that rope over a precipice. Wouldn't you then first discover how much you really trusted it?[222]

Through five chapters of this book, we looked at how understanding that the Eucharist is really Jesus unlocks deeper levels of belief in the mysteries of our faith. Once we understand what Jesus meant about the Eucharist, we suddenly find ourselves better able to understand what he meant about the "new covenant"; the significance of all of those bloody sacrifices throughout the Old Testament and the bloody cross in the New; why the Eucharist is key in defeating heresy both ancient and modern; how together we offer God true worship; and why Jesus and the early Christians repeatedly connected the Eucharist with bodily resurrection.

To use Lewis's term, those five chapters give us a logical case for trusting the "rope" of the Eucharist. Then, in the previous chapter, we looked at four saints who are examples of how living by the Eucharist makes it possible to accomplish things that would be impossible without divine grace. To borrow Lewis's imagery again, these were four saints (among countless others) who were empowered by the Eucharist to hang over the precipice and live.

But now comes the hard part: you've got to do it yourself. It's not enough to say that the doctrine of Eucharist makes sense or that it helps to make sense of the rest of Christianity, or that it helped *other* people live saintly lives. All of us have to hang by that rope. Or to use the more eucharistic-sounding language of the Bible, we must "taste and see that the Lord is good" (Ps. 34:8). And so in this final chapter, I want to try to address some common doubts about the Eucharist, as well as offering a few tips for how to make the Eucharist the center of your spiritual life.

DO YOU WANT THE EUCHARIST
TO BE TRUE?

I want first to address those who might still be unsure of whether to believe in the Eucharist. To them, I would ask (or you might ask), "Do you *want* the Eucharist to be true?"

Since our desires don't make something true or not, that question may seem irrelevant, but it isn't. Faith involves the intellect *and the will*. It's not just about knowing, for instance, that God must logically exist.[223] It's about the heart saying "yes" to him and desiring him. If we don't want to believe, God always gives us plenty of room—and plenty of excuses—not to believe.

This is easy to see in the case of atheists. From a purely rational perspective, atheists should want God to exist, even if they believe he doesn't. After all, the Christian claim involves an infinitely good God calling us to enjoy perfect happiness with him forever. Who wouldn't want that? And yet, people like the "anti-theist" Christopher Hitchens say things like, "I do not envy believers their faith. I am relieved to think that the whole story is a sinister fairy tale; life would be miserable if what the faithful affirmed was actually the case." He even claimed he could not "imagine anything more horrible or grotesque" than "cradle-to-grave divine supervision," arguing that "it would be worse, in a way, if the supervision was benign."[224]

This is nonsensical, if we're thinking rationally. Nothing is more horrible or grotesque than infinite goodness? But it *is* tremendously revealing about Hitchens's heart, and the irrationality of some unbelievers' hatred of God.

Perhaps we can even see something of this in our own lives as Christians. Logically, we should want the Eucharist to be really Jesus, even if we believe it isn't. After all, the Trinitarian God is inherently relational, and we are made in his image. We are made for relationship with him and with one another, and the whole of Christianity involves living those relationships faithfully and well (cf. Matt. 22:35–40). This desire of the heart is expressed in the language of seeing God. As the Psalmist proclaims, "Thy face, Lord, do I seek" (Ps. 27:8). We have a deep hunger for God, and a hunger to *look* upon God. And the great Christian promise is that "when he appears we shall be like him, for we shall see him as he is" (1 John 3:2).

The Eucharist fulfills our spiritual longing in a unique way, beyond anything else offered on Earth. In the Eucharist, we both look upon Christ and commune with him bodily. Through the Eucharist, we are drawn into deeper communion with our neighbor. In the words of St. Francis de Sales, it is the "center of the Christian religion, heart of devotion, and soul of piety, the ineffable mystery that comprises within itself the deepest depths of divine charity, the mystery in which God really gives himself and gloriously communicates his graces and favors to us."[225] Who wouldn't want *that?*

Of course, my argument isn't that the Eucharist must be true because it sounds good. It's simply that if we find ourselves opposed to the idea of the Eucharist, or hoping the Catholic claim isn't true, or happy that we think it isn't true, this reveals something about our own hearts.

THE ROOM WHERE GOD IS

Those of us who believe that the Eucharist is really Jesus have to examine our own hearts and lives, too.

Some time ago, I met a man who had once worked for a Western intelligence agency. He was embedded in a majority-Muslim country, posing as a businessman. Given the lawlessness of parts of the country, he had to be driven across it in the dead of night to avoid bandits. As they were speeding dangerously across the desert, with the headlights off, his driver—a Muslim who had no idea of his true identity—suddenly asked, "What are you *doing* here?"

The man froze: had his cover been blown? He replied, "What?" and the driver repeated, "What are you *doing* here?"

"What do you mean?"

The driver then explained, "You told me that you are a Catholic, yes? And you believe that in your church, there is a room where God is. I'm a Muslim, but if I believed that there was a room where God was, *I would never leave it.* So what are you doing in this country?"

We can imagine Jesus asking each of us the same question of wherever we are instead of being with him: "What are you doing here?" If we really believe Jesus is present in the Blessed Sacrament, do our actions reflect that? Do we make the time we should to be with Jesus at Mass? Or what about eucharistic adoration? There really *is* "a room where God is." Why don't we spend more time there?

EUCHARISTIC DRYNESS AND DISTRACTION

I think that there are a few ways we might answer the question of why we don't spend more time with Jesus in the Eucharist. One reason is because of spiritual dryness. The Eucharist doesn't always seem to "do" much for us, and so it's easy to choose to spend our time elsewhere. We would do well to learn from the prophet Elijah, who sought the Lord's presence not in "the great and strong wind," or the earthquake, or the fire, but in listening for the "still small voice" (1 Kings 19:11-13). Likewise, Mother Teresa's spiritual journey shows us that it's okay if we don't get a wave of spiritual consolation or a brilliant theological insight every time we go to prayer. She experienced spiritual darkness, and feelings of worthlessness and abandonment by God, even in front of the Blessed Sacrament. And yet she kept coming back faithfully anyway, a faithfulness that Our Lord rewarded abundantly.

Of course, it's easier to show up for anything, including adoration, if it's emotionally enriching rather than a spiritual struggle. But being spiritually nourished by Christ in the Eucharist doesn't always feel like being emotionally uplifted. Emotions aren't the point of prayer.

Francis de Sales points out that "a child will weep tenderly when it sees its mother bled by the lancet," but if his mother asks him for "the apple or the piece of candy he holds in his hand, he won't part with it."[226] We, too, might weep tenderly at the spear lancing the side of Christ, but "why do we not give him our heart, the sole apple of love that this dear Savior asks from us?"[227]

Conversely, as Fr. Eugene Boylan points out, our most rewarding prayer may turn out to have been in those times where we came away feeling like we had been too distracted:

> If we could only realize how much this continual turning back to God shows him our real love for him and pleases him more than that rapt attention that has its roots in selflove, we should never be

dissatisfied with our prayer on account of its numerous distractions. [. . .] We should be very greatly surprised if we could get a glimpse at the account book that the recording angel keeps, and see the different values he sets on our various attempts at prayer. The prayer that pleased us, and with which we were well satisfied, would often be quite low in his estimate, while the prayer that disgusted us, which was apparently made up of nothing but distractions, might be found to have won a very high degree of his approval.[228]

Marriage isn't made of continual Hallmark movie moments, and the most important moments in marriage may have been times that seemed ordinary or even stressful. The same is true with our relationship with Jesus: the greatest encounters with Jesus are often the ones without any fireworks.

This doesn't mean we shouldn't fight dryness and distractions as we can. If there's something causing spiritual dryness (like a sinful attachment or a lack of spiritual attentiveness), let God uproot it. When distractions come, don't give in to them, but turn back to God with humility and gratitude. But don't let their existence—which is perfectly ordinary—discourage you from spending time with Jesus in the Eucharist.

KNOWING WHAT TO SAY

A related difficulty is that we often don't know what to say or do when we go to pray. An hour (or even fifteen minutes) in front of the silent monstrance can feel like an eternity (and not in a good way) if we're kneeling or sitting there, awkwardly waiting for the time to pass. It's tempting to spend the time in "adoration" not really adoring at all, but doing other things, like spiritual reading (I've even seen people reading the church bulletin!). I don't want to criticize any of this unnecessarily because it's better than not showing up. But Jesus wants to give us more. And what does God want from us? In a word, prayer.

Brief spiritual reading can be good as a sort of icebreaker, particularly if we're physically or emotionally exhausted when we kneel down to pray. It can turn our thoughts toward the life and person of Jesus or can give us something to ponder and to discuss with God. But we should avoid letting spiritual reading *replace* prayer, because it's no substitute.

St. Josemaría Escrivá, the founder of Opus Dei, once said, "You say that you don't know how to pray? Put yourself in the presence of God, and once you have said, 'Lord, I don't know how to pray!' rest assured that you have begun to do so."[229] At that point, simply talk to him about whatever's on your heart: "about him, about yourself: joys, sorrows, successes and failures, noble ambitions, daily worries, weaknesses! And acts of thanksgiving and petitions: and love and reparation. In a word: to get to know him and to get to know yourself: 'to get acquainted!'"[230]

Formulaic prayers (like the Our Father, or the rosary, or litanies) can be helpful, so long as we're actually praying them rather than merely reciting.* When the disciples asked Jesus how to pray, remember, he gave them a formulaic

---

* If you're struggling to find the right words to say to get started, in the appendix I've included a few "warmup prayers" before the Blessed Sacrament.

prayer (Luke 11:1-4). But he also invites us to other kinds of prayer. "During vocal prayer," says Francis de Sales,

> if you find your heart drawn and invited to interior or mental prayer, don't refuse to take it up. Let your mind turn very gently in that direction and don't be concerned at not finishing the vocal prayers you intended to say. The mental prayer you substitute for them is more pleasing to God and more profitable for your soul.[231]

If Jesus is trying to show you something or tell you something, don't be afraid to put down your rosary and leave your list to go with him.

That may even mean praying before the Blessed Sacrament in a wordless way. The Curé of Ars, St. John Vianney, knew a farmer who would spend hours sitting or kneeling before the Blessed Sacrament. The priest asked him, "What do you say to Our Lord in those long visits you pay him every day and many times a day?" to which the farmer replied, "I say nothing to him. I look at him and he looks at me."[232]

The *Catechism* calls this type of prayer *contemplative prayer*, and explains how to prepare for it:

> Entering into contemplative prayer is like entering into the eucharistic liturgy: we "gather up" the heart, recollect our whole being under the prompting of the Holy Spirit, abide in the dwelling place of the Lord which we are, awaken our faith in order to enter into the presence of him who awaits us. We let our masks fall and turn our hearts back to the Lord

who loves us, so as to hand ourselves over to him as
an offering to be purified and transformed (2711).

Ultimately, prayer of this style is a gift from God that
he initiates, not something that we can simply "do" on our
own steam. All we can do is prepare our hearts to receive
this gift and accept it when it's offered.

THE GOD WHO COMES IN WEAKNESS

It might seem strange to read that "the Eucharist is at the
root of every form of holiness," particularly if we're thinking of the Eucharist as just one more devotion to add to a
list of pious exercises (*Sacramentum Caritatis* 94). But the Eucharist isn't just a way of drawing close to God, a particular
mode of praying that might help us. The Eucharist *is* God,
who has drawn near to us. And this shows us something
strange—and hopeful—about God.

Jesus entered history as a baby, placed in a manger, in the
little town of Bethlehem (Matt. 2:1; Luke 2:12). The town
is so named from the Hebrew *Bēṯ Leḥem*, "house of bread,"
and called in Arabic *Bayt Laḥm*, "house of meat."[233] Even in
that first gesture of laying him in a lowly food trough (for
that's what a manger is), we already have hints of the eucharistic nature of Jesus' incarnation.

But the shock of the Incarnation pales in comparison
to the scandal of "Christ crucified, a stumbling block to
Jews and folly to Gentiles" (1 Cor. 1:23). Jesus foretold that
"I, when I am lifted up from the earth, will draw all men
to myself" (John 12:32). That's the language of a kingly
(even heavenly) exaltation, but Jesus clearly connects this
"lifting up" with the way Moses "lifted up the serpent in

the wilderness," by mounting it upon a pole (Num. 21:8-9; John 3:14-15). So, Jesus' throne is the cross, above which are emblazoned the words "Jesus of Nazareth, the King of the Jews" (19:19).

Perhaps it shouldn't surprise us, then, to find that the same God-King who comes to us as an infant and as a condemned criminal also comes to us under the appearances of bread and wine. In each case, beneath that weakness, the eyes of faith can perceive a wellspring of divine power. And in coming to know Jesus in this way, in coming to know him as he truly is, we're formed to live out the lives of holiness God has planned for us, even in our own weakness.

ITE, MISSA EST

Finally, if the Eucharist is the key to our own spiritual lives, that can't be limited only to when we're physically in front of the Blessed Sacrament. Eucharistic devotion that stops at the door of the church is stunted and incomplete, as is a spiritual life that begins and ends with Sunday Mass.

The word *Mass* comes from the concluding Latin words of the eucharistic liturgy: *ite, missa est.* Originally, *missa* simply meant "dismissal." The priest was announcing that the liturgy was complete, and the congregation was "dismissed." But as Pope Benedict XVI explains, "in Christian usage it gradually took on a deeper meaning. The word 'dismissal' has come to imply a 'mission.'* These few words succinctly express the missionary nature of the Church" (*Sacramentum Caritatis* 51).

As the saints show us, recognizing Jesus in the Eucharist must help us to recognize him in our neighbor, and partly

---

* *Dismiss, mission, missionary,* etc., all stem from the same Latin root.

in the "least of these." This is true in the theology of grace: Jesus strengthens us through the sacrament of his body and blood. But Benedict points out that it's true in another way as well: "The Eucharist makes us discover that Christ, risen from the dead, is our contemporary in the mystery of the Church, his body. Of this mystery of love we have become witnesses" (*Sacramentum Caritatis* 97).

The good news of Easter is that Jesus Christ, who his followers thought was dead, is alive. The good news of the Eucharist is that Jesus Christ, who many of his followers think has left us for heaven, is still present on earth. The Eucharist is really Jesus, and that good news needs to be proclaimed. Once you realize that there's a room where God is, once you've tasted and seen the Lord's goodness in the sacrament of his body and his blood, once you've been equipped by Christ to recognize him in your neighbor, it's time to act.

Eucharistic Prayers

If you find yourself not knowing what to say while you're in prayer before Jesus in the Eucharist, here are a few prayers that might help you to get started. We'll look at three types: prayers before Communion, prayers after Communion, and prayers during eucharistic adoration. If these are helpful, feel free to use them. If they're not, there are any number of prayer books that can aid you in this area.[234]

PRAYERS BEFORE COMMUNION

The first set of prayers are ones to pray in *preparation for receiving* the Eucharist. These are typically prayed before Mass, although you might commit a shorter prayer to memory so you can pray it as you're going up for Communion. For instance, here's St. Thomas Aquinas's prayer before Mass, which is directed to God the Father:

> Almighty and ever-living God, I approach the sacrament of your only-begotten Son our Lord Jesus Christ, I come sick to the doctor of life, unclean to the fountain of mercy, blind to the radiance of eternal light, and poor and needy to the Lord of heaven and earth.

Lord, in your great generosity, heal my sickness, wash away my defilement, enlighten my blindness, enrich my poverty, and clothe my nakedness. May I receive the bread of angels, the King of kings and Lord of lords, with humble reverence, with the purity and faith, the repentance and love, and the determined purpose that will help to bring me to salvation. May I receive the sacrament of the Lord's body and blood, and its reality and power.

Kind God, may I receive the body of your only-begotten son, our Lord Jesus Christ, born from the womb of the Virgin Mary, and so be received into his mystical body and numbered among his members.

Loving Father, as on my earthly pilgrimage I now receive your beloved son under the veil of a sacrament, may I one day see him face to face in glory, who lives and reigns with you forever. Amen.

An eleventh-century Benedictine monk named John of Fécamp wrote a series of prayers before Mass, one for each day.[235] Each is beautiful, but my favorite is this one, originally intended for Saturdays:

I entreat thee, O Lord, by this most holy mystery of thy body and blood with which we are daily fed and given to drink, are washed and sanctified in thy Church, and are made worthy partakers of the one supreme divinity, grant unto me thy holy virtues, that filled by them I may draw near to thine altar with a good conscience. May these heavenly sacraments be made unto me salvation and life, for as thou hast said with thy holy and blessed mouth, "The bread that I will give is my flesh, which I will give for the life of the world. I am the living bread which came down from heaven. If any man eat of this bread, he shall live forever."

Sweetest Bread, heal the palate of my heart that I may taste the pleasant savor of thy love. Heal it of all infirmities that I may find sweetness in nothing other than thee. O purest Bread, having all delight and all savor, which ever refreshes us and never fails, let my heart feed on thee and may my inmost soul be fulfilled with the sweetness of thy savor. The angels feed upon thee fully: let the wayfaring man feed on thee according to his measure, that, refreshed with such a viaticum,* he may not fall by the way.

Holy Bread, O living Bread, O pure Bread, who came down from heaven and gives life unto the world, come into my heart, and cleanse me from all defilement of flesh and spirit. Enter into my soul: heal and cleanse me within and without; be the protection and continual health of my soul and body. Drive far from me all foes that lie in wait; let them flee at the presence of thy power, so that being guarded without and within by thee, I may come to thy kingdom straight away: where, not as now

---

* Viaticum ("food for the journey") is another name for the Eucharist—particularly when received by those who are nearing the end of their earthly lives.

in mysteries, but face to face, we shall behold thee: when thou shalt have delivered up the kingdom to God, the Father, and shalt be God, all in all. Then shalt thou satisfy me with thyself in wondrous fullness, so that I shall never hunger nor thirst any more. Who with the same God the Father and the Holy Spirit lives and reigns forever and ever. Amen.

In the Byzantine liturgy celebrated by Eastern Catholics, there's a beautiful prayer before communion that's part of the liturgy itself:

O Lord, I believe and profess that you are truly
    Christ,
The Son of the living God, who came into the
    world
To save sinners, of whom I am the first.

Accept me today as a partaker of your mystical
    supper, O Son of God,
For I will not reveal your mystery to your enemies,
Nor will I give you a kiss as did Judas,
But like the thief I profess to you:

Remember me, O Lord, when you come in your kingdom.
Remember me, O Master, when you come in your
    kingdom.
Remember me, O Holy One, when you come in your
    kingdom.

May the partaking of your Holy mysteries, O Lord,
Be not for my judgment or condemnation,
But for the healing of my soul and body.

O Lord, I also believe and profess, that this,
Which I am about to receive,
Is truly your most precious Body, and your
life-giving Blood,
Which, I pray, make me worthy to receive
For the remission of all my sins and for life everlast-
ing. Amen.

O God, be merciful to me, a sinner.
O God, cleanse me of my sins and have mercy on
me.
O Lord, forgive me for I have sinned without
number.

If you're looking for something shorter (and easier to memorize), St. Josemaría Escrivá was fond of this simple prayer:

I wish, my Lord and my God, to receive you with the purity, humility and love with which your Most Holy Mother received You, and with the fervor and spirit of the Saints.[236]

But more important than any particular prayer is the right attitude of heart. As Escrivá puts it, "When you approach the Tabernacle remember that he has been awaiting you for twenty centuries."[237]

If you're not able to receive Jesus in the Eucharist— whether it's because you're not yet fully in the Catholic Church, or you need to go to Confession before you can receive him, or some other reason—a pious practice is to make what's called a "spiritual communion." (These prayers became very popular during the COVID pandemic, as most Catholics were unable to attend Mass). Probably the most popular spiritual communion prayer goes like this:

> My Jesus, I believe that you are present in the most holy sacrament. I love you above all things, and I desire to receive you into my soul. Since I cannot at this moment receive you sacramentally, come at least spiritually into my heart. I embrace you as if you were already there and unite myself wholly to you. Never permit me to be separated from you. Amen.

PRAYERS AFTER MASS

In his book *The Spirit of the Liturgy,* then–Cardinal Joseph Ratzinger stressed the importance of a time of silent prayer after receiving Jesus in Holy Communion. He describes this time as "the moment for an interior conversation with the Lord who has given himself to us, for that essential 'communicating,' that entry into the process of communication, without which the external reception of the sacrament becomes mere ritual and therefore unfruitful." While acknowledging that this is often difficult (particularly if the church isn't quite), he nevertheless encourages that "whenever possible, this silence after Communion should be used, and the faithful should be given some guidance for interior prayer."[238]

For many Catholics, this time of interior prayer continues even after the Mass itself has ended, and many of the other congregants have left the church. In the words of St. Josemaría, "Do not leave the church almost immediately after receiving the sacrament. Surely you have nothing so important on that you cannot give our Lord ten minutes to say thanks."[239]

If staying *isn't* possible, you can practice maintaining this holy silence and time with God after you've left the church by, for instance, keeping the radio off when you get in the car. If you're looking for good prayers to offer during this time, Aquinas has a prayer after Mass that pairs nicely with his prayer before Mass:

> Lord, Father all-powerful and ever-living God, I thank You, for even though I am a sinner, your un-profitable servant, not because of my worth but in the kindness of your mercy, You have fed me with the precious body and blood of your son, our Lord Jesus Christ.
>
> I pray that this Holy Communion may not bring me condemnation and punishment but forgiveness and salvation.
>
> May it be a helmet of faith and a shield of good will. May it purify me from evil ways and put an end to my evil passions. May it bring me charity and patience, humility and obedience, and growth in the power to do good. May it be my strong defense against all my enemies, visible and invisible, and the perfect calming of all my evil impulses, bodily and spiritual. May it unite me more closely to you, the one true God, and lead me safely through death to everlasting happiness with you.

And I pray that you will lead me, a sinner, to the banquet where you, with your son and the Holy Spirit, are true and perfect light, total fulfillment, everlasting joy, gladness without end, and perfect happiness to your saints. Grant this through Christ our Lord. Amen.

Many Catholics pray the *Anima Christi*, popularized by St. Ignatius of Loyola, after receiving Communion. It goes like this:

Soul of Christ, sanctify me.
Body of Christ, save me.
Blood of Christ, inebriate me.
Water from the side of Christ, wash me.
Passion of Christ, strengthen me.
O Good Jesus, hear me.
Within your wounds hide me.
Separated from you, let me never be.
From the evil one, defend me.
At the hour of my death, call me
And close to you, bid me,
That with your saints I may praise you
Forever and ever. Amen.

St. Ignatius also wrote many prayers of his own, including the *Suscipe*, a prayer entrusting oneself entirely to Jesus. Given the eucharistic context, in which Jesus gives us himself, it is fitting that we should respond by offering him all of ourselves:

Take, Lord, and receive all my liberty, my memory, my understanding, and my entire will—all that I have and possess. You, Lord, have given all that to me. I now give it back to you, O Lord. All of it is yours. Dispose of it according to your will. Give me love of yourself along with your grace, for that is enough for me.[240]

PRAYERS DURING EUCHARISTIC ADORATION

Finally, if you wish to adore Jesus outside of Mass (for instance, in eucharistic adoration), there are a variety of helpful prayers. During private prayer in front of the Eucharist, I find it helpful to begin by reminding myself that I'm in the presence of God, by praying something like this prayer (from St. Josemaría):

My Lord and my God, I firmly believe that you are here; that you see me, that you hear me. I adore you with profound reverence; I beg your pardon for my sins, and the grace to make this time of prayer fruitful.

My Immaculate Mother, St. Joseph my father and lord, my guardian angel, intercede for me. Amen.

In contrast, if you're worshiping Jesus in the Eucharist in a more formal or group setting, there's a good chance that there will be prayers and hymns already incorporated. Many of these were written by Thomas Aquinas for the feast of

Corpus Christi, at the request of Pope Urban IV. These are worth reading through prayerfully, because they're theologically and spiritually rich. Take, for instance, the *Adoro Te Devoto*. There are various English versions, but I appreciate the English poet Gerard Manley Hopkins's translation:

> Godhead, I adore thee fast in hiding; thou
> God in these bare shapes, poor shadows, darkling
>   now:
> See, Lord, at thy service low lies here a heart
> Lost, all lost in wonder at the God thou art.
>
> Seeing, touching, tasting, are in thee deceived;
> How says trusty hearing? *That* shall be believed:
> What God's Son has told me, take for truth I do;
> Truth himself speaks truly or there's nothing true.
>
> On the cross thy godhead made no sign to men;
> Here thy very manhood steals from human ken;*
> Both are my confession, both are my belief,
> And I pray the prayer of the dying thief.
>
> I am not like Thomas, wounds I cannot see,
> But can plainly call thee Lord and God as he:
> This faith each day deeper be my holding of,
> Daily make me harder hope and dearer love.
>
> O thou our reminder of Christ Crucified,

---

* *Ken* means "sight" or "knowledge." Aquinas is saying that we couldn't *see* that Jesus on the cross was God, but needed to rely upon faith. Now, we don't see him even as man (in the way we see one another) but take his human and divine presence by faith.

Living Bread the life of us for whom he died,
Lend this life to me then: feed and feast my mind,
There be thou the sweetness man was meant to
    find.

Like what tender tales tell of the Pelican;
Bathe me, Jesus Lord, in what thy bosom ran—
Blood that but one drop of has the worth to win
All the world forgiveness of its world of sin.

Jesus, whom I looked at veiled here below,
I beseech thee send me what I thirst for so,
Some day to gaze on thee face to face in light
And be blest for ever with thy glory's sight.

Another of his hymns is *O Salutaris Hostia*, frequently sung at the beginning of eucharistic adoration. It's actually part of a larger poem, but we typically just pray the final two verses:

O saving victim opening wide
The gate of heaven to all below.
Our foes press on from every side;
Thine aid supply, thy strength bestow.

To thy great name be endless praise
Immortal Godhead, one in three;
Oh, grant us endless length of days,
In our true native land with thee.

But perhaps the most famous hymn Aquinas wrote on the Eucharist is the *Pange Lingua,* which St. John Paul II called "a profound meditation on the Eucharistic mystery."[241] It begins:

> Sing, my tongue, the Savior's glory,
> of his flesh the mystery sing;
> of the blood, all price exceeding,
> shed by our immortal king,
> destined, for the world's redemption,
> from a noble womb to spring.

Although the full hymn is six stanzas, typically only the final two (beginning *Tantum Ergo* in Latin) are prayed in adoration:

> Down in adoration falling,
> Lo! the sacred host we hail;
> Lo! o'er ancient forms departing,
> newer rites of grace prevail;
> faith for all defects supplying,
> where the feeble sense fail.

> To the everlasting Father,
> and the Son who reigns on high,
> with the Holy Ghost proceeding
> forth from each eternally,
> be salvation, honor, blessing,
> might and endless majesty.
> Amen. Alleluia.

If you prefer something simpler, many Catholics will quietly pray this prayer:

O sacrament most holy, O sacrament divine!

All praise and all thanksgiving be every moment
thine!

About the Author

Joe Heschmeyer is a staff apologist for Catholic Answers. A popular author, speaker, blogger, and podcaster, he holds a bachelor's degree in philosophy from Kenrick-Glennon Seminary in St. Louis and a baccalaureate in sacred theology from Rome's Pontifical University of St. Thomas Aquinas (Angelicum). His books include *Pope Peter* and *The Early Church Was the Catholic Church*. Joe resides with his wife, Anna, and their children in the Kansas City area.

Endnotes

1   Cf. Eusebius, *Church History*, 4, 22, NPNF 2/1:199.

2   Greek philosophers and scientists knew that the earth was round centuries before the time of Christ, and their view of the world was widely accepted by later Christian thinkers. But the ancients miscalculated the size of the earth, and believed that the sun, planets, and stars revolved around the earth. But although this Ptolemaic model was mathematically sophisticated and fairly successful, its predictions never *perfectly* matched up with reality. Even the ancient Greeks realized this, recognizing that certain heavenly bodies seemed to "wander" across the sky. They named them *asteres planētai*, or "wandering stars." Today, we simply call them "planets." Over the centuries, the small discrepancies between model and reality that the Greeks had noticed grew larger and larger, requiring constant tweaking to the Ptolemaic model until Copernicus finally pointed out that perhaps it was the model itself that was the problem. Copernicus proposed an alternative theory (*heliocentrism*) that was simpler, more elegant, and did a better job of explaining things. My point in that just as brilliant geocentrists could provide possible explanations for the astrological data, brilliant Protestant theologians can provide possible explanations for the biblical data about the Eucharist. But in both cases, there's a simpler and more elegant explanation that doesn't require so many exegetical backflips.

3   C.S. Lewis, "Is Theology Poetry?" in *The Weight of Glory* (New York: HarpersCollins, 2001), p. 140.

4   Some Lutherans reject the term *consubstantial* for their eucharistic

views.

5   There is some confusion within Lutheranism over whether to worship the Eucharist, and Luther left it up to believers' individual judgment, although he argued that "I really think it would be better to follow the example of the apostles and not worship, than to follow our custom and worship. Not that adoration is wrong, but simply because there is less danger in not adoring than in adoring." See "Luther and adoration of the sacrament," WELS (Wisconsin Evangelical Lutheran Synod), available at wels.net.

6   Cyril of Jerusalem, *Lecture 22*, 9 (*On the Mysteries*, 4, 9), NPNF 2/7:152.

7   Cyril, *Lecture 22*, 1, NPNF 2/7:151.

8   This was the crux of the objection of Berengarius of Tours, who in the eleventh century became one of the first Christians to challenge the Real Presence. See Lawrence Feingold, *The Eucharist: Mystery of Presence, Sacrifice, and Communion* (Steubenville: Emmaus Academic, 2018), pp. 238-239.

9   This is similar to the error made by Celsus, one of the earliest pagan critics of Christianity, when he assumed that the Incarnation meant that God had "abandoned the heavenly regions," leaving heaven ungoverned to dwell on the earth. Cf. Origen, *Against Celsus*, book 4, ch. 28, *ANF* 4:508.

10 I'm indebted to Gavin Ortlund for this expression, who drew it from the writings of the Reformer John Calvin. It's true that Jesus "emptied himself, taking the form of a servant, being born in the likeness of men" (Phil. 2:7), but he didn't (and couldn't) stop being God, or stop being in heaven. As one of the early Christians explained, in becoming man, Jesus "had not lost his former being, but he had become what he was not before; he had not abdicated his own position, yet he had taken ours; he prays that the nature which he had assumed may be promoted to the glory which he had never renounced" (see Hilary of Poitiers, *De Trinitate* 3, 16, NPNF 2/9:66).

11 I'm indebted to Cardinal Timothy Dolan for the "history, mystery, and majesty" formulation (from his book with John L. Allen, Jr., *A People of Hope*). Dolan is paraphrasing Fr. Pius Parsch (1884-1954),

who spoke of Christ's threefold advent:"the first in the flesh as
Man; the second in majesty and glory on the last day; and the third
in grace."

12 For an excellent brief history of why the Church defined transubstantiation, and what the two erroneous misinterpretations of
it were, I recommend Brett Salkeld, "Transubstantiation Isn't a
Disconnected Doctrine," *Church Life Journal*, November 13, 2019.

13 Mary Rodgers, *Freaky Friday* (New York: Scholastic Book Services,
1972), p. 1.

14 For instance, Eusebius, a Church historian living in the fourth
century, explains that after Matthew, Mark, and Luke "had already
published their Gospels, they say that John, who had employed
all his time in proclaiming the Gospel orally, finally proceeded to
write for the following reason. The three Gospels already mentioned having come into the hands of all and into his own too, they
say that he accepted them and bore witness to their truthfulness;
but that there was lacking in them an account of the deeds done
by Christ at the beginning of his ministry" (*Church History* 24, 7,
NPNF 2/1:153).

15 Craig Keener points out that the fact "that the multitudes must
'recline' (6:10) may suggest an allusion to the Passover (6:4). For
normal meals people sat on chairs, but they reclined at banquets
and festivals in accordance with the Greek custom probably adopted during the Hellenistic period." Craig S. Keener, *The Gospel of
John: A Commentary*, vol. 1 (Grand Rapids: Baker Academic, 2003),
p. 666. So the Passover (and the Last Supper) offers an appropriate
lens through which we should make sense of John 6.

16 F.F. Bruce, *The Gospel of John: Introduction, Exposition and Notes*
(Grand Rapids: Wm. B. Eerdmans Publishing Co., 1983), p. 159.

17 Ibid.

18 *NIV Matthew Henry Commentary in One Volume: Based on the Broad
Oak Edition*, ed. Leslie F. Church (Grand Rapids: Zondervan, 1992),
p. 345.

19 J.C. Ryle, *Expository Thoughts on the Gospels: St. John, Vol. 1* (London: Wm. Hunt and Co., 1856), p. 396. Ryle says that "the opinion

here expressed may startle some who have not looked closely into the subject," so he seems to realize his argument seems to be an implausible reading of Jesus' words.

20 Bruce, p. 145. Although Bruce notes that this fact "in itself would not require a eucharistic significance for the feeding," this point doesn't stand alone, but is part of a broader constellation of evidence pointing toward a eucharistic reading of John 6.

21 D.A. Carson, *The Gospel According to John* (Grand Rapids: Wm. B. Eerdmans Publishing Co., 1991), p. 281.

22 Carson, p. 277.

23 The pagan Caecilianus claims, for instance, that Christians eat infants "covered over with meal" and "lick up its blood" (Minucius Felix, *Octavius* 8, ANF 4:177-178).

24 We find this way of referring to the Old Testament even before Christ. For instance, 2 Maccabees 15:9 refers to "the law and the prophets." Even today, Jews refer to their scriptures as the *TaNaKH*, a Hebrew acronym for the Law, the Prophets, and "the Writings." This third category is a sort of catch-all for inspired books that aren't legal texts or prophetic literature, like the Psalms, Proverbs, Ruth, and Esther..

25 Daniel Lynwood Smith, *Into the World of the New Testament: Greco-Roman and Jewish Texts and Contexts* (London: Bloomsbury, 2015), p. 10.

26 Ratzinger, *Many Religions—One Covenant*, p. 48.

27 Victor H. Matthews, *Old Testament Themes* (Eugene: Wipf and Stock, 2017), p. 7.

28 Protestants sometimes distinguish between those who take a "covenantal" and those who take a "dispensational" view, but there are other hermeneutical frameworks, like the Lutheran distinction between "Law" and "Gospel." See Paul Enns, *The Moody Handbook of Theology* (Chicago: Moody Publishers, 2014), p. 495 ff; Kenneth Hagen, "From Testament to Covenant in the Early Sixteenth Century," *The Sixteenth Century Journal*, vol. 3, no. 1 (April 1972), pp. 1-24. Historically, the "covenantal" view is associated with Reformed Protestantism, also known as Calvinism.

29 Charles Spurgeon, "Not Sufficient and Yet Sufficient," in *The Met-ropolitan Tabernacle Pulpit*, vol. 36 (London: Passmore & Alabaster, 1890), pp. 467-468.

30 J.I. Packer, "On Covenant Theology," in *Revelations of the Cross* (Peabody, Mass.: Hendrickson Publishers, 1998), p. 10.

31 Scott Hahn, "Foreword," in *Many Religions—One Covenant*, p. 14.

32 Peter J. Gentry and Stephen J. Wellum, *Kingdom Through Covenant: A Biblical-Theological Understanding of the Covenants*, 2nd ed. (Wheaton: Crossway, 2012), p. 162.

33 Kwakkel argues against the view that "*berith* stands for the rela-tionship between two persons or between God and his people itself," arguing instead that "it seems more appropriate to say that *berith* denotes the agreement or convention that is at the base of a relationship or regulates it" ("Berith and Covenants in the Old Testament: A Contribution to a Fruitful Cooperation of Exegesis and Systematic Theology," in *Covenant: A Vital Element of Reformed Theology* (Leiden: Brill, 2022), p. 36).

34 Raymond C. Ortlund, Jr., *Proverbs: Wisdom that Works* (Wheaton: Crossway, 2012), p. 90.

35 Ratzinger, *Many Religions—One Covenant*, pp. 76-77.

36 Packer, p. 10.

37 Ibid.

38 "The paradigm of the covenant, central to Israel's self-understand-ing and Paul's background, is inherently relational." Samuel D. Ferguson, *The Spirit and Relational Anthropology in Paul*, p. 140.

39 Scott Hahn, *Swear to God: The Promise and Power of the Sacraments* (New York: Doubleday, 2004), p. 61.

40 "Contracts also tend to be more impersonal because they cover the exchange of goods and services, whereas covenants involve agree-ments between people particularly where the persons themselves become the substance of the alliance. The virtue of justice operates to insure contracts; the virtue of love and fidelity guarantees cove-nants" (David M. Thomas, Christian Marriage: A Journey Together (Collegeville: Liturgical Press, 1983), p. 103).

41 Scott and Kimberly Hahn, *Rome Sweet Home* (San Francisco: Ignatius Press, 1993), p. 30.

42 Richard A. Norris, Jr., *The Song of Songs: Interpreted by Early Christian and Medieval Commentators* (Grand Rapids: Wm. B. Eerdmans Publishing, 2003), p. xviii, (explaining that "the ancient interpreters of the Song of Songs, Jews and Christians, treat the love lyrics *allegorically*; that is, they treat human love-affairs—vividly described, with scarcely veiled scenes of seduction and happy allusions to certain of the arts of love—as signifying the love between God and the people of God, or between the Word and Wisdom of God and the human soul."

43 Smith, p. 11.

44 Robert Simpson, *An Atheist in the Choir Loft* (Xlibris, 2012), pp. 148-49.

45 Christopher Hitchens, *God is Not Great: How Religion Poisons Everything* (Toronto: McClelland & Stewart Ltd., 2007), p. 208.

46 Sam Harris, *Letter to a Christian Nation* (New York: Vintage Books, 2008), pp. 93, 96.

47 This account comes from the sixteenth-century Dominican friar Diego Durán, and is quoted at length in Davíd Carrasco, *City of Sacrifice: The Aztec Empire and the Role of Violence in Civilization* (Boston: Beacon Press, 1999), p. 20. For a long time, many scholars dismissed the stories of Aztec human sacrifice as Spanish propaganda. But then, explains David Roos, "In 2015 and 2018, archeologists working at the Templo Mayor excavation site in Mexico City discovered proof of widespread human sacrifice among the Aztecs—none other than the very skull towers and skull racks that conquistadors had described in their accounts" ("Human Sacrifice: Why the Aztecs Practiced This Gory Ritual," *History*, October 11, 2018, available at history.com).

48 Lest you think I'm intentionally choosing fringe figures, a *Christianity Today* article from 2008 traced the growth in Calvinism among Evangelicals in part to the influence of "popular pastors such as John Piper, R.C. Sproul, and John MacArthur" (Ken Walker, "TULIP Blooming," *Christianity Today*, January 17, 2008).

49 John MacArthur, *The Murder of Jesus* (Nashville: Nelson Books, 2004), p. 220.

50 John Piper, *Future Grace: The Purifying Power of the Promises of God*, rev. ed. (Colorado Springs: Multnomah Books, 2012) p. 110; John MacArthur, "Who Killed Jesus?," *Grace to You*, July 10, 2009, available at gty.org.

51 This is from R.C. Sproul's sermon at the 2008 *Together for the Gospel* Conference in Louisville, Kentucky, which is available on YouTube. Additionally, a copy of the transcript (with commentary) is available at Tim Challies, "How R.C. Sproul Blessed the Church by Preaching the Curse," Challies, May 22, 2018, available at challies.com.

52 John Calvin, *Institutes of the Christian Religion*, book 2, ch. 16, trans. Henry Beveridge (Peabody, MA: Hendrickson Publishers, 2008), p. 331.

53 Caren Teves, "Response to 'the Leash,'" in *Bullets into Bells: Poets & Citizens Respond to Gun Violence*, eds. Brian Clements, Alexandra Teague, and Dean Rader (Boston: Beacon Press, 2017), p. 111.

54 Dan Elliott and Sadie Gurman, "Remembering the Aurora theater shooting victims," *Coloradoan*, July 16, 2015.

55 Patrick Saunders, "Aurora theater shooting: Illinois sailor John Larimer was youngest of five children," *Denver Post*, July 21, 2012.

56 Ryan Grenoble, "'Dark Knight' Shooting: 3 Boyfriends Die Shielding Girlfriends During Aurora Massacre," *Huffington Post*, July 23, 2012.

57 Thomas Aquinas, *Summa Theologiae*, III, 48, 2, c.

58 Ibid.

59 Max L. Stackhouse, "The Moral Meanings of Covenant," *The Annual of the Society of Christian Ethics*, vol. 16 (1996), p. 250.

60 Daniel J. Elazar, *Covenant and Polity in Biblical Israel: Biblical Foundations and Jewish Expressions*, vol. 1 of *Covenant Tradition in Politics* (London: Routledge, 2017), p. 64.

61 Elazar, p. 66.

62 Elazar, pp. 136–37.

63 William K. Gilders, *Blood Ritual in the Hebrew Bible: Meaning and Power* (Baltimore: John Hopkins Press, 2004), p. 39.

64 Ibid.

65 G. Henton Davies, *Exodus* (London: SCM Press, 1967), p. 194, quoted by Gilders, pp. 39-40.

66 Roger Oakland, *Another Jesus?: The Eucharistic Christ and the New Evangelization*, 2nd. ed.(Eureka, MT: Lighthouse Trails Publishing, 2020), p. 54.

67 Brant Pitre, "Jesus, the Messianic Banquet, and the Kingdom of God," *Letter & Spirit*, vol. 5 (2009), p. 150 (emphasis omitted).

68 Quran 4:157, *English Translation of the Holy Quran*, trans. Maulana Muhammad Ali, ed. Zahid Aziz (Wembley, UK: Ahmadiyya Anjuman Lahore Publications, 2010), pp. 133-134.

69 "[Suleiman] Mourad concludes that while there is complete agreement amongst Muslim exegetes that Jesus was not crucified, there is no unity as to who died in his place. Some argue God made someone look like Jesus, and that person was crucified, although again there is no agreement as to who that person was. A less popular view is that one of Jesus' disciples volunteered to take his place, and was made to look like Jesus" (Tom Wilson, *Prophetic Precursors: Pointers Toward Muhammad or Christ?* (Eugene, OR: Wipf and Stock, 2020), p. 204).

70 *Against Heresies*, 3, 3, ANF 1:416.

71 On Cerinthus's theology, see Charles E. Hill, "Cerinthus, Gnostic or Chiliast?: A New Solution to an Old Problem," *Journal of Early Christian Studies*, vol. 8, no. 2 (Summer 2000), pp. 135-172.

72 As Roger Olsen explains, "In a nutshell, they believed that matter, including the body, is an inherently limiting prison or even evil drag on the good soul or spirit of the human person and that the spirit is essentially divine—'spark of God' dwelling in the tomb of the body" (*The Story of Christian Theology: Twenty Centuries of Tradition & Reform* (Downers Grove: InterVarsity Press, 1999), p. 29).

73 So, for instance, St. Augustine says that "there is no need, therefore, that in our sins and vices we accuse the nature of the flesh to the

injury of the Creator, for in its own kind and degree the flesh is good" (*City of God*, 14, 5, NPNF 1/2:265).

74 "Certain Gnostics denied the incarnation: if Christ was a divine, eternal and perfect being, he could not have become flesh, as matter was evil and impure" (Clare Goodrick-Clarke and Nicholas Goodrick-Clarke, *G.R.S. Mead and the Gnostic Quest*, ed. Clare Goodrick-Clarke and Nicholas Goodrick-Clarke (Berkeley: North Atlantic Books, 2005), p. 143).

75 G.R.S. Mead, "The Secret of Jesus," The Theosophical Review 43 (September 1908–February 1909), pp. 323-334, in *G.R.S. Mead and the Gnostic Quest*, pp. 166-167.

76 The Cathars, descendants of the Gnostics, shared the view that "there must be two creative powers, a good and a bad one; the good one created all good things, the evil one all bad things. So there is a good creation and a bad creation The good creation is spiritual, invisible, and eternal; it is the world of God and participates in the divine nature. It is from the spiritual world that the soul has come down. The bad creation is material, visible, and corruptible" (Roelof van den Broek, "The Cathars: Medieval Gnostics?" in *Gnosis and Hermeticism from Antiquity to Modern Times*, eds. Roelof van den Broek and Wouter J. Hanegraaff (Albany: State University of New York, 1998), p. 90).

77 On the resurgence of Gnosticism in modern Evangelicalism, see Abigail Rine Favale, "Evangelical Gnosticism," *First Things*, May 2018, describing her own experience teaching students at George Fox University; Philip J. Lee also spotted this spiritual danger in his 1993 book *Against the Protestant Gnostics* (Oxford: Oxford University Press). Although this problem is acute within Evangelicalism, it's not the case that all Protestants (or even all Evangelicals) are influenced by Gnosticism. Neither is it the case that only Evangelicals are influenced by Gnosticism. *All* Christians should be aware of the way that bad views of the body may have colored how we view ourselves as well as sin and redemption.

78 John Calvin, *Institutes of the Christian Religion*, 1, 15, trans. Henry Beveridge (Peabody: Hendrickson Publishers, 2008), p. 105.

79 "According to Gnostic thinking, the immortal soul is a prisoner of the mortal body. Some Gnostics coined the slogan *sōma sēma*: The *sōma* (the body) is a *sēma* (a tomb) for the soul" (Leander E Keck, *Echoes of the Word* (Cambridge: Lutterworth Press, 2015), p. 69).

80 Trevin Wax, "Luther vs. Zwingli 6: Flesh and Spirit," The Gospel Coalition, February 15, 2008, available at thegospelcoalition.org.

81 Paul Althaus, *The Theology of Martin Luther*, trans. Robert C. Schultz (Philadelphia: Fortress Press, 1966), p. 395.

82 *City of God*, 14, 3, NPNF 1/2:264.

83 *Tractate 27 on John*, 5, NPNF 1/7:175.

84 Charles Haddon Spurgeon (1834–1892) is remembered as the "Prince of Preachers" for good reason. By his thirtieth birthday, Spurgeon's sermons were already selling at a rate of about a million copies a year. He is, in short, "one of evangelical Christianity's immortals," and by no means a fringe figure (Carl F.H. Henry, "Introduction," in Lewis A. Drummond, *Spurgeon: Prince of Preachers* (Grand Rapids: Kregel Publications, 1992), p. 11).

85 Charles Spurgeon, "Sermon No. 653: A Blow for Puseyism," October 8, 1865, p.2, available at spurgeongems.org.

86 Ibid.

87 Augustine points out that "he who extols the nature of the soul as the chief good, and condemns the nature of the flesh as if it were evil, assuredly is fleshly both in his love of the soul and hatred of the flesh; for these his feelings arise from human fancy, not from divine truth" (*City of God*, NPNF 1/2:265). The great irony, then, is that by appealing to human intelligence rather than the authority of Christ, Spurgeon is behaving in a "fleshly" way.

88 Spurgeon, "A Blow for Puseyism," p. 2.

89 Spurgeon, "Sermon No. 2544: The One and the Many," August 3, 1884, p. 2, available at spurgeongems.org.

90 *Against Heresies*, 3, 11, ANF 1:426.

91 Hannah Peckham, "'You Don't Have a Soul': C.S. Lewis Never Said It," Mere Orthodoxy, July 5, 2012, available at mereorthodoxy. com. One of the first to use something like this quotation was long

before C.S. Lewis: the Anglican Rev. Dr. R. Thornton, in an 1881 address to the Church of England's Church Congress, in which he tries to show the common ground between Christianity and Spiritualism.

92 C.S. Lewis, *Mere Christianity* (New York: HarperOne, 2000), p. 64.

93 It's also telling when Evangelicals quote Lewis on this point but scrub his eucharistic references. For instance, Joe Rigney renders the quotation as "God never meant man to be a purely spiritual creature. … He likes matter. He invented it." Joe Rigney, *Lewis on the Christian Life: Becoming Truly Human in the Presence of God* (Wheaton: Crossway, 2018), p. 108.

94 Spurgeon, "A Blow for Puseyism," p. 2.

95 *Letter to the Smyrnaeans* 7, ANF 1:89.

96 Ibid.

97 *Against Heresies*, 4, 18, ANF 1:486.

98 *The Great Catechism* 38, NPNF 2/5:504.

99 C.S. Lewis, *The Screwtape Letters* (San Francisco: Harper San Francisco, 2001), p. 37.

100 Advanced Life Support Group, *Advanced Pediatric Life Support: A Practical Approach to Emergencies*, 6th ed. (Oxford: John Wiley & Sons, 2016), p. 313.

101 *The Great Catechism* 37, NPNF 2/5:504.

102 Ibid.

103 *Great Catechism* 37, NPNF 2/5:505.

104 John Calvin, *Institutes of the Christian Religion*, book 4, ch. 18, trans. Henry Beveridge (Grand Rapids: Wm. B. Eerdmans Publishing Co., 1989), p. 607.

105 James F. White, *Protestant Worship: Traditions in Transition* (Louisville: Westminster John Knox Press, 1989), p. 14.

106 O.S. Hawkins, *The Pastor's Guide to Leading and Living* (Nashville: Thomas Nelson, 2012), p. 24.

107 Barry Liesch, *People in the Presence of God: Models and Directions for Worship* (Grand Rapids: Zondervan, 1988), p. 99.

108 "While some scholars support a definition of the 'synagogue' as a type of Greco-Roman association, others define it as a Jewish public institution derived from earlier city gate assemblies. There are merits to both definitions, which are each supported by distinct sets of evidence" (Jordan J. Ryan, *The Role of the Synagogue in the Aims of Jesus*, p. 34).

109 Reuven Hammer, *Entering Jewish Prayer: A Guide to Personal Devotion and the Worship Service* (New York: Schocken books, 1994), p. 61.

110 Lester L. Grabbe, a historian of early Judaism, writes that "it is natural that people often assume that Judaism in the Second Temple period was more or less like contemporary Judaism, in which people meet weekly or even more frequently in synagogues to pray, worship, and hear the Bible read. The written scripture and its reading and study are assumed to be the focus of Judaism at all times." But as Grabbe points out, "the Judaism of pre-70 times was formally structured in a quite different way from the Judaism of later times" (*An Introduction to Second Temple Judaism: History and Religion of the Jews in the Time of Nehemiah, the Maccabees, Hillel and Jesus* (London: T&T Clark, 2010), p. 40).

111 O. Wesley Allen, Jr., *Protestant Worship: A Multisensory Introduction for Students and Practitioners* (Nashville: Abingdon Press, 2019), pp. 20-21.

112 James W. McKinnon, "On the Question of Psalmody in the Ancient Synagogue," *Early Music History*, vol. 6 (1986), p. 171.

113 McKinnon, p. 170.

114 McKinnon, p. 171.

115 Everett Ferguson, *Worship, Eucharist, Music, and Gregory of Nyssa*, vol. 3 of *The Early Church at Work and Worship* (Eugene: Cascade, 2017), p. 14. See also Ingvild Sælid Gilhus, *Animals, Gods and Humans: Changing Attitudes to Animals in Greek, Roman and Early Christian Thought* (London: Routledge, 2006).

116 Mike Smith, "Tiny Samaritan community marks Passover sacrifice as numbers grow," *Times of Israel*, April 19, 2019.

117 Robert J. Daly, "The Power of Sacrifice in Ancient Judaism and

Christianity," *Journal of Ritual Studies*, vol. 4, no. 2 (Summer 1990), p. 181. Daly's description is supported by the biblical evidence, which included specialized ritual sacrifices for various purposes. For instance, "If it is the anointed priest who sins, thus bringing guilt on the people," the priest is to offer "a young bull without blemish to the Lord for a sin offering"; but if the sinner is the king, he's to instead offer a male goat; and if he's an ordinary person, his sin offering is a female goat (Lev. 4:3, 22-23, 27-28).

118 Bava Batra 4a, *The William Davidson Talmud*, available at sefaria.org.

119 Loraine Boettner, *Roman Catholicism* (Phillipsburg: Presbyterian and Reformed Publishing Co., 1962), p. 274.

120 Joseph Ratzinger, *Pilgrim Fellowship of Faith: The Church as Communion*, eds. Stephan Otto Horn and Vinzenz Pfnür, trans. Henry Taylor (San Francisco: Ignatius Press, 2005), pp. 110-111.

121 Robert E. Webber, *Ancient-Future Faith: Rethinking Evangelicalism for a Postmodern World* (Grand Rapids: Baker books, 1999), p. 98.

122 Ibid.

123 I explore this in greater detail in my book *The Early Church was the Catholic Church* (El Cajon: Catholic Answers, 2021), pp. 85-94.

124 This argument is often rooted in faulty history. For instance, Paul Basden claims that between 587 B.C. and 4 B.C., "sacrifice and music all but disappeared" in Israel's worship, and "keeping the Torah in all its detail became the goal of worship" (*Exploring the Worship Spectrum: Six Views*, ed. Paul A. Basden (Grand Rapids: Zondervan, 2004), p. 14). The New Testament description of Israel's worship, in contrast, is that "every priest stands daily at his service, offering repeatedly the same sacrifices, which can never take away sins" (Heb. 10:11).

125 David Hamshire, *Hebrew Foundations of the Christian Faith* (Eugene: Wipf & Stock, 2019), p. 103.

126 Ronald P. Byars, *The Future of Protestant Worship: Beyond the Worship Wars* (Louisville: Westminster John Knox Press, 2002), p. 44.

127 Marianne Meye Thompson is right to say that Jesus' answer to the Samaritan woman "constitutes neither a polemic against

external ritual and forms of worship, nor an argument in favor
of the interiorization of worship, nor a criticism of the idea of
'sacred space' per se." Instead, "it is rather "a reorientation of one's
worship through and in the presence of God in the messianic
temple, Jesus" ("Reflections on Worship in the Gospel of John,"
The Princeton Seminary Bulletin, vol. 19, no. 3 (1998), pp. 268-269).

128 *Third Instruction* 17-18. Many of the other Church Fathers say
similar things. Indeed, a sacramental reading of John 19:34 is
shared by figures as diverse as Martin Luther, John Calvin, J.B.
Lightfoot, and Rudolph Boltmann. See Sebastian A. Carnazzo,
Seeing Blood and Water: a Narrative-Critical Study of John 19:34
(Eugene, OR: Pickwick Publications, 2012), pp. 1-8, 36-38, and
76-81.

129 "God took the rib of Adam and formed a woman, so Christ gave
us blood and water from his side and formed the Church." John
Chrysostom, *Third Instruction*.

130 *City of God*, 10, 6, NPNF 1/2:184.

131 *City of God*, 10, 6, NPNF 1/2:184.

132 Second Vatican Council, *Sacrosanctum Concilium* 47, December 4,
1963.

133 *Against Heresies*, 4, 18, ANF 1:486.

134 *Letter to the Ephesians* 20, ANF 1:58.

135 *Letter to the Smyrnaeans* 7, ANF 1:89.

136 Hans Urs von Balthasar once lamented that "only a very small
number of initiates have read and are aware of Gregory of Nyssa,
and they have jealously guarded their secret," which he considered an unfitting obscurity for "the most profound Greek
philosopher of the Christian era," and a theologian who St.
Maximilian the Confessor dubbed "the Universal Doctor." Hans
Urs von Balthasar, *Presence and Thought: An Essay on the Religious
Philosophy of Gregory of Nyssa*, trans. Mark Sebanc (San Francisco:
Ignatius Press, 1995), p. 15. As von Balthasar points out, the Sec-
ond Council of Nicaea referred to Gregory not just as a Church
Father, but as the "Father of Fathers."

137 *Great Catechism* 37, NPNF 2/5:505.

138 Ibid.

139 David C. Kraemer, *Jewish Eating and Identity Through the Ages* (London; Routledge, 2009), p. 52.

140 *Great Catechism* 37, NPNF 2/5:505-506.

141 *On the Mysteries* 9, 50, NPNF 2/10:324.

142 *On the Mysteries* 9, 51-52, NPNF 2/10:324.

143 *On the Mysteries* 9, 53, NPNF 2/10:324.

144 C.S. Lewis, *Miracles: A Preliminary Study* (London: HarperCollins-Publishers, 2002), pp. 218-219. .

145 Lewis, *Miracles*, p. 219.

146 Cf. C.S. Lewis, "Introduction," in Athanasius, *On the Incarnation* (Crestwood, NY: St.Vladimir's Orthodox Theological Seminary, 1953), p. 9.

147 Lewis, *Miracles*, p. 222.

148 *Great Catechism* 37, NPNF 2/5:504.

149 *Ibid.,* NPNF 2/5:506.

150 Ibid.

151 Ratzinger refers here to a passage from Augustine's *Confessions*. Another translation reads, "I am the food of strong men; grow, and thou shalt feed upon me; nor shall thou convert me, like the food of thy flesh, into thee, but thou shall be converted into me."

152 Joseph Ratzinger, "Lecture by H.E. Cardinal Ratzinger at the Bishops' Conference of the Region of Campania in Benevento (Italy) on the Topic: 'Eucharist, Communion And Solidarity,'" June 2, 2002, available at vatican.va.

153 Augustine, *Sermon 228B*, 3, in *Sermons (184–229z) on the Liturgical Seasons*, ed. John E. Rotelle, trans. Edmund Hill, vol. III/6 of *The Works of Saint Augustine: A Translation for the 21st Century* (New Rochelle, NY: New City Press, 1993), p. 262.

154 As Pope St. John Paul II explains, the celebration of the Eucharist "cannot be the starting-point for communion; it presupposes that communion already exists, a communion which it seeks

to consolidate and bring to perfection." John Paul II, *Ecclesia de Eucharista* 35, April 17, 2003. We can no more switch the order of baptism and Eucharist than we could switch the order of the wedding ceremony and the wedding night.

155 *Against Heresies*, 5, preface, ANF 1:526.

156 *On the Incarnation of the Word*, 54, NPNF 2/4:65.

157 Michael Peppard, *The Son of God in the Roman World: Divine Sonship in its Social and Political Context* (Oxford: Oxford University Press, 2011), pp. 46-47.

158 St. Peter speaks about "the knowledge of God and of Jesus our Lord," and then refers to "his" divine power (2 Pet. 1:2-3). As Thomas R. Schreiner points out, "when Peter referred to 'his divine power,' it is difficult to know whether he referred to God or Christ. . . . The ambiguity in the text indicates that Peter did not clearly distinguish between God and Christ. We can conclude from this that God and Christ were venerated equally." Thomas R. Schreiner, *1, 2 Peter, Jude*, vol. 37 of *The New American Commentary* (Nashville: B&H Publishing Group, 2003), p. 291. This conclusion is reinforced by the fact, just two verses prior, Peter refers to Jesus as "our God and Savior Jesus Christ."

159 *Against Heresies*, 3, 19, ANF 1:448.

160 *First Apology* 21, ANF 1:170.

161 Joseph Smith, "King Follett Sermon, April 7, 1844," quoted in Rulon T. Burton, *We Believe: Doctrines and Principles of the Church of Jesus Christ of Latter-day Saints* (Salt Lake City: Tabernacle books, 2004), p. 351.

162 Spencer W. Kimball, ". . . the Matter of Marriage, Oct. 22, 1976," quoted in *Doctrines of the Gospel: Student Manual* (Salt Lake City: The Church of Jesus Christ of Latter-day Saints, 2010), p. 29.

163 Elder Lorenzo Snow, "At Brigham City Tabernacle, prior to being sentenced by Judge Powers in the First District Court, Jan. 10, 1886," quoted in *We Believe*, p. 351.

164 *Discourse III Against the Arians* 19, NPNF 2/4:404.

165 C.S. Lewis, *The Weight of Glory: And Other Addresses* (New York,

NY: HarperOne, 2001), p. 45.

166 "For by no other means could we have attained to incorruptibility and immortality, unless we had been united to incorruptibility and immortality." Irenaeus, *Against Heresies*, 3, 19, ANF 1:448-449.

167 *Catechetical Lecture 22*, 3, NPNF 2/7:151.

168 *Letter 61*, 2, NPNF 2/4:578-579.

169 *Great Catechism 37*, NPNF 2/5:506.

170 Ibid.

171 *Against Heresies*, 5, 2, ANF 1:528.

172 Ibid.

173 Bonnie J. Rough, "The Birdmen," *The Iowa Review,* vol. 36, no. 3 (2006), p. 33. doi: https://doi.org/10.17077/0021-065X.6173.

174 Michael Abrams, *Birdmen, Batmen, and Skyflyers: Wingsuits and the Pioneers Who Flew in Them, Fell in Them, and Perfected Them* (New York: Three Rivers Press, 2006), p. 36.

175 Rough, p. 33.

176 Joe Rhatigan, *Inventions that Could Have Changed the World . . . But Didn't!* (Watertown, MA: Charlesbridge, 2015), p. 18.

177 Joseph Ratzinger with Vittorio Messori, *The Ratzinger Report*, trans. Salvator Attanasio and Graham Harrison (San Francisco: Ignatius Press, 1986), pp. 129-130.

178 Ibid.

179 Ibid.

180 Ibid.

181 Ambrose, *Death of Satyrus*, 1, 46, NPNF 2/10:168.

182 Ambrose, *Death of Satyrus*, 1, 47-48, NPNF 2/10:168-169.

183 "It is estimated that he converted approximately 30,000 souls as opposed to the hagiographical number of one million attributed to him." Pamila Gupta, "'Signs of Wonder': The Postmortem Travels of Francis Xavier in the Indian Ocean World," in *Indian Ocean Studies: Cultural, Social, and Political Perspectives*, eds. Shanti Moorthy and Ashraf Jamal (New York: Routledge, 2010), p. 215, fn.

21. The 30,000 figure is, if anything, low. Ultimately, "how many converts Xavier made is left to the educated guesswork of history. The numbers go as high as one million, but modern scholars peg the number around 30,000, while the Jesuits claim 700,000" (Mark Galli and Ted Olsen, *131 Christians Everyone Should Know* (Nashville: Christianity Today, 2000), p. 238).

184 Kelsie Stewart, "Francis Xavier's Mission to Japan (1549), in *Great Events in Religion: An Encyclopedia of Pivotal Events in Religious History*, vol. 3, eds. Florin Curta and Andrew Holt (Santa Barbara: ABC-CLIO, 2017), p. 745.

185 Henry James Coleridge, in *The Life and Letters of St. Francis Xavier*, vol. 2 [hereafter "*Letters*"] (London: Burns and Oates, 1872), p. 46.

186 Ibid.

187 "Letter 89, To Master Simon Rodriguez," *Letters*, pp. 375-376.

188 "Letter 105, To Father Simon Rodriguez, in Portugal," *Letters*, p. 490.

189 To get around this, the monks wrote in Latin, and their writings were translated into Japanese by a young Japanese Methodist, who ended up converting to Catholicism and joining their community. See Sergio C. Lorit, *The Last Days of Maximilian Kolbe* (Brooklyn: New City Press, 1981), pp. 122.

190 Dariusz Żuk-Olszewski, "Missionary Work and Methods of Catechization of St. Maximilian Maria Kolbe in Japan," in *Theory of the Religious and Art Education in Contemporary Research*, eds. Tomáš Jablonský and Dušan Kováč-Petrovský (Milan: EduCATT, 2013), p. 196; Lorit, pp. 120-124.

191 Desmond Forristal, "Maximilian Kolbe," *The Furrow*, vol. 28, no. 10 (October 1977), p. 630.

192 Forristal, p. 630.

193 Jerzy Domański, *For the Life of the World: Saint Maximilian and the Eucharist*, trans. Peter D. Fehlner (New Bedford: Academy of the Immaculate, 1999), p. 116.

194 Forristal, p. 629.

195 John Paul II, *Address of the Holy Father John Paul II to the Franciscan Sisters of the Immaculate* 3, June 15, 2000.

196 Diana Dewar, *Saint of Auschwitz: The Story of Maximilian Kolbe* (San Francisco: Harper & Row, 1982), p. 106.

197 As Dewar notes, "priests came second to Jews in Hitler's hate-list. Each transport to Auschwitz concentration camp was greeted by the SS officer in charge of new prisoners with the words; 'If there are Jews in the transport, they cannot live more than two weeks, if there are priests, they may live one month, the rest three months.'" Diana Dewar, *Saint of Auschwitz: The Story of Maximilian Kolbe* (San Francisco: Harper & Row, 1982), p. 95. This account is corroborated by Forristal, p. 633, who names the SS officer as the Karl Fritzsch.

198 Lorit, p. 138.

199 Quoted in Dewar, p. 109.

200 Dewar, pp. 111-112.

201 John W. Primomo, *Architect of Death at Auschwitz: A Biography of Rudolf Höss* (Jefferson, NC: McFarland & Co., 2020), p. 115.

202 Quoted in Volker Koop, *The Commandant of Auschwitz: Rudolf Höss* (Yorkshire: Pen & Sword books, 2001), p. 148.

203 *Letter to the Romans* 4, ANF 1:75.

204 *Letter to the Romans* 7, ANF 1:76-77.

205 Frank Newport, "Mother Teresa Voted by American People as Most Admired Person of the Century," Gallup, December 31, 1999, available at news.gallup.com..

206 Kenneth J. Cooper, "Solemn Farewell to Mother Teresa," *Washington Post*, September 13, 1997. "Cardinal Sodano, the Vatican secretary of state, said the funeral Mass before 13,000 in the sports arena and an international television audience of millions." In addition to ten Catholic cardinals, some "400 foreign delegates from two dozen countries" attended the funeral, including "first lady Hillary Clinton; Italian president Oscar Luigi Scalfaro; Albanian president Rexhep Mejdani; Canadian prime minister Jean Chretien; Bangladeshi prime minister Sheikh Hasina; Jordan's Queen Noor; Belgium's Queen Fabiola; Spain's Queen Sofia; British deputy prime minister John Prescott, and the duchess of Kent."

207 Navin Chawla, "The Mystery of Mother Teresa," *The Hindu*, August 25, 2009.

208 Daniel Stacey, "In India, Teresa Draws Devotees of All Faiths," *Wall Street Journal*, September 2, 2016.

209 *Address of His Holiness Benedict XVI*, December 26, 2010.

210 Quoted in Mary Poplin, "Radical Marxist, Radical Womanist, Radical Love: What Mother Teresa Taught Me About Social Justice," in *A Place for Truth: Leading Thinkers Explore Life's Hardest Questions*, ed. Dallas Willard (Downers Grove: InterVarsity Press, 2010), p. 282.

211 John Paul II, *Letter of the Holy Father John Paul II on the Occasion of the 50th Anniversary of the Foundation of the Missionaries of Charity* ["*MC Letter*"], October 2, 2000.

212 For a nuanced view of her early years, see Gëzim Alpion, *Mother Teresa: Saint or Celebrity?* (Abingdon: Routledge, 2007).

213 Mother Teresa, "Letter of the Foundress," quoted by John Paul II, *MC Letter*.

214 Dominique Lapierre, *The City of Joy*, trans. Kathryn Spink (Garden City, NY: Doubleday & Co., 1985), pp. 229-230.

215 Poplin, p. 292.

216 Mark Newmeyer, Benjamin Keyes, Sonji Gregory, Kamala Palmer, Daniel Buford, Priscilla Mondt and Benjamin Okai, "The Mother Teresa Effect: The Modulation of Spirituality in using the CISM Model with Mental Health Service Providers," *International Journal of Emergency Mental Health and Human Resilience*, vol. 16, no. 1 (2014), p. 17. doi: 10.4172/1522-4821.1000104.

217 Navin Chawla, *Mother Teresa*, centenary ed. (New Dehli: Penguin, 2003), p. 180.

218 Mother Teresa, *Come Be My Light: The Private Writings of the Saint of Calcutta*, ed. Brian Kolodiejchuk (New York: Doubleday, 2007), p. 210.

219 *Come Be My Light*, p. 216.

220 "*Christianity Today* asked more than 100 of its contributors and church leaders to nominate the ten best religious books of the

twentieth century. …. By far, C.S. Lewis was the most popular author and *Mere Christianity* the book nominated most often. Indeed, we could have included even more Lewis works, but finally we had to say: 'Enough is enough; give some other authors a chance.'" "Books of the Century," *Christianity Today*, April 24, 2000. Both Lewis and Mother Teresa were also listed among "The Ten Most Influential Christians of the Twentieth Century" by *Christian History* magazine, in its sixty-fifth issue (2000).

221 C.S. Lewis, *A Grief Observed* (New York: HarperOne, 2000), p. 23.

222 Lewis, *A Grief Observed*, pp. 22-23.

223 Fr. Wojciech Giertych (the official "theologian of the pontifical household") explains that "faith is not located uniquely in the cognitive order. It encompasses the entire person, involving also the will, which shows the intellect that it is good for it to adhere to God" (*The Spark of Faith: Understanding the Power of Reaching Out to God* (Irondale, AL: EWTN Publishing, 2018), p. 100).

224 Christopher Hitchens, *Letters to a Young Contrarian* (New York: Basic books, 2005), p. 55.

225 Francis de Sales, *Introduction to the Devout Life*, 2, 14, trans. John K. Ryan (New York: Image books, 2003), p. 92.

226 De Sales, 4, 13, p. 245.

227 De Sales, 4, 13, pp. 245-246.

228 Eugene Boylan, *Difficulties in Mental Prayer* (Westminster, MD: Newman Press, 1957), p. 56.

229 Josemaría Escrivá, *The Way* 90, in *The Way / Furrow / The Furrow* (New York: Scepter, 2001), p. 21.

230 Escrivá, *The Way* 91, p. 21.

231 De Sales, 2, 1, p. 72.

232 Alfred Monnin, *The Life of the Curé d'Ars* (London: Burns & Lambert, 1862), p. 55.

233 John Everett-Heath, *Oxford Concise Dictionary of World Place Names* (Oxford: Oxford University Press, 2005), p. 64.

234 To recommend just one such book, I've personally found

Fr. James Socias's *Handbook of Prayers* to be a great spiritual aid.

235 John of Fécamp's prayers are frequently (but falsely) credited to St. Ambrose of Milan, so you may be familiar with these under the title of "Prayers before Mass of St. Ambrose" or something similar. See Jordan Aumann, *Christian Spirituality in the Catholic Tradition* (San Francisco: Ignatius Press, 2001), p. 87.

236 Jesus Sancho, "Spiritual Communion: a Prayer that Traveled Around the World," Opus Dei, January 8, 2019, available at opusdei.org.

237 Josemaría Escrivá, *The Way* 537.

238 Joseph Ratzinger, *The Spirit of the Liturgy*, trans. John Saward (San Francisco: Ignatius Press, 2000), p. 210.

239 Josemaría Escrivá, *In Love with the Church* (New York: Scepter Publishers, 1989), p. 73.

240 Ignatius of Loyola, *The Spiritual Exercises of Saint Ignatius*, trans. George E. Ganss (Chicago: Loyola Press, 1992), p. 95.

241 John Paul II, *Homily for the Feast of Corpus Christi*, May 29, 1997.